𝔉rontenac 𝔈dition

FRANCIS PARKMAN'S WORKS

VOLUME ONE

𝕱𝖗𝖔𝖓𝖙𝖊𝖓𝖆𝖈 𝕰𝖉𝖎𝖙𝖎𝖔𝖓

Pioneers of France

in the

New World

*[France and England in North America
Part First]*

BY

FRANCIS PARKMAN

3 ✗✗00

IN TWO VOLUMES

VOLUME ONE

NEW YORK

CHARLES SCRIBNER'S SONS

1915

Printers
S. J. PARKHILL & CO., BOSTON, U.S.A.

INTRODUCTORY ESSAY.

I.

In the summer of 1865 I had occasion almost daily to pass by the pleasant windows of Little, Brown, and Co., in Boston, and it was not an easy thing to do without stopping for a moment to look in upon their ample treasures. Among the freshest novelties there displayed were to be seen Lord Derby's translation of the Iliad, Forsyth's Life of Cicero, Colonel Higginson's Epictetus, a new edition of Edmund Burke's writings, and the tasteful reprint of Froude's History of England, just in from the Riverside Press. One day, in the midst of such time-honored classics and new books on well-worn themes, there appeared a stranger that claimed attention and aroused curiosity. It was a modest crown octavo clad in sombre garb and bearing the title, "Pioneers of France in the New World." The author's name was not familiar to me, but

presently I remembered having seen it upon a
stouter volume labelled "The Conspiracy of
Pontiac," of which many copies used to stand
in a row far back in the inner and dusky regions
of the shop. This older book I had once taken
down from its shelf, just to quiet a lazy doubt
as to whether Pontiac might be the name of a
man or a place. Had that conspiracy been an
event in Merovingian Gaul or in Borgia's Italy,
I should have felt a twinge of conscience at not
knowing about it; but the deeds of feathered
and painted red men on the Great Lakes and the
Alleghanies, only a century old, seemed remote
and trivial. Indeed, with the old-fashioned
study of the humanities, which tended to keep
the Mediterranean too exclusively in the centre
of one's field of vision, it was not always easy to
get one's historical perspective correctly adjusted.
Scenes and events that come within the direct
line of our spiritual ancestry, which until yes-
terday was all in the Old World, thus become
unduly magnified, so as to deaden our sense of
the interest and importance of the things that
have happened since our forefathers went forth
from their homesteads to grapple with the
terrors of an outlying wilderness. We find no
difficulty in realizing the historic significance of

TO THE MEMORY

OF

THEODORE PARKMAN, ROBERT GOULD SHAW,
AND HENRY WARE HALL,

SLAIN IN BATTLE,

THIS VOLUME IS DEDICATED BY THEIR KINSMAN,

THE AUTHOR.

PUBLISHER'S PREFACE.

———◆———

THIS edition of the writings of Francis Parkman is issued under an arrangement with his publishers, Messrs. Little, Brown and Company, and has the approval of his family. It was prepared with the endeavor to make it the definitive edition of his works and an enduring memorial to his fame.

The text used is that of the latest edition of each work prepared for the press by the distinguished author. He carefully revised and added to several of his works, not through change of views, but in the light of new documentary evidence which his patient research and untiring zeal extracted from the hidden archives of the past. Thus he rewrote and enlarged "The Conspiracy of Pontiac;" the new edition of "La Salle and the Discovery of the Great West" (1878) and the 1885 edition of "Pioneers of France" included very important additions; and a short time before his death he added to

"The Old Régime" fifty pages, under the title of "The Feudal Chiefs of Acadia." The present edition therefore includes each work in its final state as perfected by the historian, and the indexes have been entirely re-made.

The illustrations mainly consist of authentic portraits and contemporary prints, faithfully reproduced from the originals by Messrs. Boussod, Valadon, and Co., successors to Goupil and Co., Paris. The publishers have aimed to supplement the text of the author with portraits and pictures specially described or referred to in his works, and to include portraits of the principal personages in the narrative, necessarily omitting those concerning which the authenticity of existing portraits is doubtful. They have been able to secure for the work a number of interesting portraits taken directly from the original paintings, some of which are in the possession of descendants of the personages of the histories, permission for their reproduction having been generously accorded. Several of these have not before been published.

Full information regarding the ownership and source of the subjects will be found in the list of illustrations prefixed to each volume of the present edition. The publishers desire to tender their thanks to all who have rendered assistance or who have placed pictures at their disposal, including, in addition to those mentioned in the lists of illustrations, L'Abbé H. R. Casgrain, and Mgr. C. O. Gagnon, Secrétaire des Archives, Quebec, Hon. F. G. Baby, Rev. A. E. Jones, Mr. E. L. Bond, Mr. C. T. Hart, and Mr. William Drysdale of Montreal, M. Philéas Gagnon, Quebec, Dr. F. D. Stone, Librarian of the Historical Society of Pennsylvania, Miss E. S. Parkman, Mr. George R. Barrett, and Mr. Z. T. Hollingsworth, Boston, Justin Winsor, LL.D., Cambridge, Dr. S. A. Green of the Massachusetts Historical Society, Mr. Clarence S. Bement and Mr. Charles R. Hildeburn, Philadelphia; and the following institutions and libraries : McGill University, Montreal, The Boston Public Library, The Pennsylvania Historical Society, Philadelphia, The Metropolitan Museum of Art, New York, The Château de Ramezay, and the Sisters of the Congregation of Notre Dame, Montreal, and at Quebec, Hôtel Dieu, Université Laval, Convent des Ursulines, and Hôpital Général. They are also greatly indebted to Messrs. Boussod, Valadon, and Co. for valuable aid in tracing pictures located in France and England.

Marathon and Chalons, of the barons at Runny-
mede or Luther at Wittenberg; and scarcely a
hill or a meadow in the Roman's Europe but
blooms for us with flowers of romance. Literature and philosophy, art and song, have ex-
pended their richest treasures in adding to the
witchery of Old World spots and Old World
themes.

But as we learn to broaden our horizon, the
perspective becomes somewhat shifted. It begins to dawn upon us that in New World events
there is a rare and potent fascination. Not only
is there the interest of their present importance,
which nobody would be likely to deny, but there
is the charm of a historic past as full of romance
as any chapter whatever in the annals of mankind. The Alleghanies as well as the Apennines
have looked down upon great causes lost and
won, and the Mohawk valley is classic ground no
less than the banks of the Rhine. To appreciate
these things thirty years ago required the vision
of a master in the field of history; and when I
carried home and read the " Pioneers of France,"
I saw at once that in Francis Parkman we had
found such a master. The reading of the book
was for me, as doubtless for many others, a pioneer experience in this New World. It was a

delightful experience, repeated and prolonged for
many a year as those glorious volumes came one
after another from the press until the story of
the struggle between France and England for the
possession of North America was at last completed.   It was an experience of which the full
significance required study in many and apparently diverse fields to realize.   By step after step
one would alight upon new ways of regarding
America and its place in universal history.

First and most obvious, plainly visible from
the threshold of the subject, was its extreme
picturesqueness.   It is a widespread notion that
American history is commonplace and dull; and
as for the American red man, he is often thought
to be finally disposed of when we have stigma-
tized him as a bloodthirsty demon and grovelling
beast.   It is safe to say that those who enter-
tain such notions have never read Mr. Parkman.   In the theme which occupied him his
poet's eye saw nothing that was dull or commonplace.   To bring him vividly before us, I will
quote his own words from one of the introductory pages of his opening volume: —

"The French dominion is a memory of the
past; and when we evoke its departed shades,
they rise upon us from their graves in strange

romantic guise.   Again their ghostly camp-fires seem to burn, and the fitful light is cast around on lord and vassal and black-robed priest, mingled with wild forms of savage warriors, knit in close fellowship on the same stern errand.   A boundless vision grows upon us : an untamed continent; vast wastes of forest verdure; mountains silent in primeval sleep ; river, lake, and glimmering pool; wilderness oceans mingling with the sky.   Such was the domain which France conquered for civilization.   Plumed helmets gleamed in the shade of its forests, priestly vestments in its dens and fastnesses of ancient barbarism.   Men steeped in antique learning, pale with the close breath of the cloister, here spent the noon and evening of their lives, ruled savage hordes with a mild parental sway, and stood serene before the direst shapes of death. Men of courtly nurture, heirs to the polish of a far-reaching ancestry, here with their dauntless hardihood put to shame the boldest sons of toil."

When a writer in sentences that are mere generalizations gives us such pictures as these, one has much to expect from his detailed narrative glowing with sympathy and crowded with incident.   In Parkman's books such expectations **are never** disappointed.   What was an uncouth

and howling wilderness in the world of literature
he has taken for his own domain and peopled it
forever with living figures dainty and winsome,
or grim and terrible, or sprightly and gay.
Never shall be forgotten the beautiful earnest-
ness, the devout serenity, the blithe courage of
Champlain; never can we forget the saintly
Marie de l'Incarnation, the delicate and long-
suffering Lalemant, the lion-like Brébeuf, the
chivalrous Maisonneuve, the grim and wily Pontiac, or that man against whom fate sickened of
contending, the mighty and masterful La Salle.
These, with many a comrade and foe, have now
their place in literature as permanent and sure
as Tancred or Saint Boniface, as the Cid or Robert Bruce.   As the wand of Scott revealed un-
suspected depths of human interest in Border
castle and Highland glen, so it seems that North
America was but awaiting the magician's touch
that should invest its rivers and hillsides with
memories of great days gone by.   Parkman's
sweep has been a wide one, and many are the
spots that his wand has touched, from the cliffs
of the Saguenay to the Texas coast, and from
Acadia to the western slopes of the Rocky
Mountains.

I do not forget that earlier writers than Park-

man had felt something of the picturesqueness
and the elements of dramatic force in the history
of the conquest of our continent.   In particular
the characteristics of the red men and the incidents of forest life had long ago been made the
theme of novels and poems, such as they were;
I wonder how many people of to-day remember
even the names of such books as " Yonnondio " or
" Kabaosa." "All such work was thrown into
the shade by that of Fenimore Cooper, whose
genius, though limited, was undeniable.   But
when we mention Cooper we are brought at once
by contrast to the secret of Parkman's power. "
It has long been recognized that Cooper's Indians
are more or less unreal; just such creatures never
existed anywhere.   When Corneille and Racine
put ancient Greeks or Romans on the stage they
dressed them in velvet and gold-lace, flowing
wigs, and high buckled shoes, and made them
talk like Louis XIV.'s courtiers; in seventeenth-
century dramatists the historical sense was lacking.   In the next age it was not much better.
When Rousseau had occasion to philosophize
about men in a state of nature he invented the
Noble Savage, an insufferable creature whom any
real savage would justly loathe and despise.   The
noble savage has figured extensively in modern

literature, and has left his mark upon Cooper's pleasant pages, as well as upon many a chapter of serious history. But you cannot introduce unreal Indians as factors in the development of a narrative without throwing a shimmer of unreality about the whole story. It is like bringing in ghosts or goblins among live men and women: it instantly converts sober narrative into fairy tale; the two worlds will no more mix than oil and water. The ancient and mediæval minds did not find it so, as the numberless histories encumbered with the supernatural testify; but the modern mind does find it so. The modern mind has taken a little draught, the prelude to deeper draughts, at the healing and purifying well of science; and it has begun to be dissatisfied with anything short of exact truth. When any unsound element enters into a narrative, the taint is quickly tasted and its flavor spoils the whole.

We are then brought, I say, to the secret of Parkman's power. His Indians are true to the life. In his pages Pontiac is a man of warm flesh and blood, as much so as Montcalm or Israel Putnam. This solid reality in the Indians makes the whole work real and convincing. Here is the great contrast between Parkman's work and that of Prescott, in so far as the latter dealt with American themes. In reading Prescott's account of the conquest of Mexico one feels oneself in the world of the "Arabian Nights;" indeed, the author himself in occasional comments lets us see that he is unable to get rid of just such a feeling. His story moves on in a region that is unreal to him, and therefore tantalizing to the reader; his Montezuma is a personality like none that ever existed beneath the moon. This is because Prescott simply followed his Spanish authorities not only in their statements of physical fact, but in their inevitable misconceptions of the strange Aztec society which they encountered; the Aztecs in his story are unreal, and this false note vitiates it all. In his Peruvian story Prescott followed safer leaders in Garcilasso de la Vega and Cieza de Leon, and made a much truer picture; but he lacked the ethnological knowledge needful for coming into touch with that ancient society, and one often feels this as the weak spot in a narrative of marvellous power and beauty.

Now it was Parkman's good fortune at an early age to realize that in order to do his work it was first of all necessary to know the Indian by personal fellowship and contact. It was also his good fortune that the right sort of Indians were still accessible. What would not **Prescott** have given, what would not any student of human evolution give, for a chance to pass a week or even a day in such a community as the Tlascala of Xicotencatl or the Mexico of Montezuma! That phase of social development has long since disappeared. But fifty years ago on our great western plains and among the Rocky Mountains there still prevailed a state of society essentially similar to that which greeted the eyes of Champlain upon the Saint Lawrence and of John Smith upon the Chickahominy. In those days the Oregon Trail had changed but little since the memorable journey of Lewis and Clark in the beginning of the present century. In 1846, two years after taking his bachelor degree at Harvard, young Parkman had a taste of the excitements of savage life in that primeval wilderness. He was accompanied by his kinsman, Mr. Quincy Shaw. They joined a roving tribe of Sioux Indians, at a time when to do such a thing was to take their lives in their hands, and they spent a wild summer among the Black Hills of Dakota and in the vast moorland solitudes through which the Platte River winds its interminable length. In the chase and in the wigwam, in watching the sorcery of which their religion chiefly consisted, or in listening to primitive folk-tales by the evening camp-fire, Mr. Parkman learned to understand the red man, to interpret his motives and his moods. With his naturalist's keen and accurate eye and his quick poetic apprehension, that youthful experience formed a safe foundation for all his future work. From that time forth he was fitted to absorb the records and memorials of the early explorers and to make their strange experiences his own.

The next step was to gather these early records from government archives, and from libraries public and private, on both sides of the Atlantic, — a task, as Parkman himself called it, " abundantly irksome and laborious." It extended over many years and involved several visits to Europe. It was performed with a thoroughness approaching finality. Already in the preface to the " Pioneers " the author was able to say that he had gained access to all the published materials in existence. Of his research among manuscript sources, a notable monument exists in a cabinet now standing in the library of the Massachusetts Historical Society, containing nearly two hundred folio volumes of documents copied from the originals by expert copyists. Ability to incur heavy expense is, of course, a

prerequisite for all undertakings of this sort, and
herein our historian was favored by fortune.
Against this chiefest among advantages were to
be offset the hardships entailed by delicate health
and inability to use the eyes for reading and writing.   Mr. Parkman always dictated instead of
holding the pen, and his huge mass of documents
had to be read aloud to him.   The heroism shown
year after year in contending with physical ailments was the index of a character fit to be
mated, for its pertinacious courage, with the
heroes that live in those shining pages.

• The progress in working up materials was slow
and sure.   "The Conspiracy of Pontiac," which
forms the sequel and conclusion of Parkman's
work, was first published in 1851, only five years
after the summer spent with the Indians.   Fourteen years then elapsed before the "Pioneers"
made its appearance in Little, Brown, and Co.'s
window; and then there were yet seven-and-
twenty years more before the final volumes came
out in 1892.   Altogether about half a century
was required for the building of this grand literary monument.   Nowhere can we find a better
illustration of the French critic's definition of a
great life, — a thought conceived in youth and
realized in later years.

This elaborateness of preparation had its share
in producing the intense vividness of Mr. Parkman's descriptions.   Profusion of detail makes
them seem like the accounts of an eye-witness.
The realism is so strong that the author seems
to have come in person fresh from the scenes he
describes, with the smoke of the battle hovering
about him and its fierce light glowing in his
eyes.   Such realism is usually the prerogative of
the novelist rather than of the historian, and in
one of his prefaces Mr. Parkman recognizes that
the reader may feel this and suspect him.   " If
at times," he says, " it may seem that range has
been allowed to fancy, it is so in appearance
only; since the minutest details of narrative or
description rest on authentic documents or on
personal observation." [1]

This kind of personal observation Mr. Parkman carried so far as to visit all the important
localities, indeed well-nigh all the localities, that
form the scenery of his story, and study them
with the patience of a surveyor and the discern-
ing eye of a landscape painter.   His strong love
of nature added keen zest to this sort of work.
From boyhood he was a trapper and hunter; in
later years he became eminent as a horticulturist,

[1] See page c.

originating new varieties of flowers. To sleep
under the open sky was his delight. His books
fairly reek with the fragrance of pine woods. I
open one of them at random, and my eye falls
upon such a sentence as this: "There is soft-
ness in the mellow air, the warm sunshine, and
the budding leaves of spring; and in the forest
flower, which, more delicate than the pampered
offspring of gardens, lifts its tender head through
the refuse and decay of the wilderness." Looking at the context, I find that this sentence comes
in a remarkable passage suggested by Col.
Henry Bouquet's western expedition of 1764,
when he compelled the Indians to set free so
many French and English prisoners. Some of
these captives were unwilling to leave the society
of the red men; some positively refused to accept
the boon of what was called freedom. In this
strange conduct, exclaims Parkman, there was no
unaccountable perversity; and he breaks out with
two pages of noble dithyrambics in praise of savage life. "To him who has once tasted the reckless independence, the haughty self-reliance, the
sense of irresponsible freedom, which the forest
life engenders, civilization thenceforth seems flat
and stale. . . . The entrapped wanderer grows
fierce and restless, and pants for breathing-room.

His path, it is true, was choked with difficulties, but his body and soul were hardened to meet them ; it was beset with dangers, but these were the very spice of his life, gladdening his heart with exulting self-confidence, and sending the blood through his veins with a livelier current. The wilderness, rough, harsh, and inexorable, has charms more potent in their seductive influence than all the lures of luxury and sloth. And often he on whom it has cast its magic finds no heart to dissolve the spell, and remains a wanderer and an Ishmaelite to the hour of his death." [1]

No one can doubt that the man who could write like this had the kind of temperament that could look into the Indian's mind and portray him correctly. But for this inborn temperament all his microscopic industry would have availed him but little. To use his own words, " Faithfulness to the truth of history involves far more than a research, however patient and scrupulous, into special facts. Such facts may be detailed with the most minute exactness, and yet the narrative, taken as a whole, may be unmeaning or untrue." These are golden words for the student of the historical art to ponder. To make a truthful record of a vanished age, patient

[1] Pontiac, iii. chap. xxvii.

scholarship is needed, and something more. **Into**
the making of a historian there should enter something of the philosopher, something of the naturalist, something of the poet. In Parkman this
rare union of qualities was realized in a greater
degree than in any other American historian.
Indeed, I doubt if the nineteenth century can
show in any part of the world another historian
quite his equal in respect of such a union.

There is one thing which lends to Parkman's
work a peculiar interest, and will be sure to
make it grow in fame with the ages. Not only
has he left the truthful record of a vanished
age so complete and final that the work will
never need to be done again, but if any one
should in future attempt to do it again he cannot approach the task with quite such equipment
as Parkman. In an important sense the age of
Pontiac is far more remote from us than the
age of Clovis or the age of Agamemnon. When
barbaric society is overwhelmed by advancing
waves of civilization, its vanishing is final; the
thread of tradition is cut off forever with the
shears of Fate. Where are Montezuma's Aztecs?
Their physical offspring still dwell on the table-
land of Mexico and their ancient speech is still
heard in the streets, but that old society is as

extinct as the trilobites, and has to be painfully studied in fossil fragments of custom and tradition. So with the red men of the North; it is not true that they are dying out physically, as many people suppose, but their stage of society is fast disappearing, and soon it will have vanished forever. Soon their race will be swallowed up and forgotten, just as we overlook and ignore to-day the existence of five thousand Iroquois farmers in the State of New York.

Now, the study of comparative ethnology has begun to teach us that the red Indian is one of the most interesting of men. He represents a stage of evolution through which civilized men have once passed, — a stage far more ancient and primitive than that which is depicted in the Odyssey or in the Book of Genesis. When Champlain and Frontenac met the feathered chieftains of the St. Lawrence, they talked with men of the Stone Age face to face. Phases of life that had vanished from Europe long before Rome was built survived in America long enough to be seen and studied by modern men. Behind Mr. Parkman's picturesqueness, therefore, there lies a significance far more profound than one at first would suspect. He has portrayed for us a wondrous and forever fascinating

stage in the evolution of humanity. We may
well thank Heaven for sending us such a scholar,
such an artist, such a genius, before it was too
late.   As we look at the changes wrought in the
last fifty years, we realize that already the oppor-
tunities by which he profited in youth are in
large measure lost.   He came not a moment too
soon to catch the fleeting light and fix it upon
his immortal canvas.

' Thus Parkman is to be regarded as first of all
the historian of Primitive Society.   No other
great historian has dealt intelligently and con-
secutively with such phases of barbarism as he
describes with such loving minuteness.   To the
older historians all races of men very far below
the European grade of culture seemed alike; all
were ignorantly grouped together as " savages."
Mr. Lewis Morgan first showed the wide difference between true savages, such as the Apaches
and Bannocks on the one hand, and barbarians
with developed village life like the Five Nations
and the Cherokees.   The latter tribes in the
seventeenth and eighteenth centuries exhibited
social phenomena such as were probably witnessed about the shores of the Mediterranean
some seven or eight thousand years earlier.   If
we carry our thoughts back to the time that saw

the building of the Great Pyramid, and imagine civilized Egypt looking northward and eastward upon tribes of white men with social and political ideas not much more advanced than those of Frontenac's red men, our picture will be in its most essential features a correct one. What would we not give for a historian who, with a pen like that of Herodotus, could bring before us the scenes of that primeval Greek world before the cyclopean works at Tiryns were built, when the ancestors of Solon and Aristides did not yet dwell in neatly joinered houses and fasten their door-latches with a thong, when the sacred city-state was still unknown, and the countryman had not yet become a bucolic or " tender of cows," and butter and cheese were still in the future. No written records can ever take us back to that time in that place, for there, as everywhere in the eastern hemisphere, the art of writing came many years later than the domestication of animals and some ages later than the first building of towns. But in spite of the lack of written records, the comparative study of institutions, especially comparative jurisprudence, throws back upon those prehistoric times a light that is often dim but sometimes wonderfully suggestive and instructive. It is a light that reveals among primeval Greeks ideas and customs essentially similar to those of the Iroquois. It is a light that grows steadier and brighter as it leads us to the conclusion that five or six thousand years before Christ white men around the Ægean Sea had advanced about as far as the red men in the Mohawk valley two centuries ago. The one phase of this primitive society illuminates the other, though extreme caution is necessary in drawing our inferences. Now Parkman's minute and vivid description of primitive society among red men is full of lessons that may be applied with profit to the study of pre-classic antiquity in the Old World. No other historian has brought us into such close and familiar contact with human life in such ancient stages of its progress. In Parkman's great book we have a record of vanished conditions such as hardly exists anywhere else in all literature.

I say his great book, using the singular number, for with the exception of that breezy bit of autobiography, "The Oregon Trail," all Parkman's books are the closely related volumes of a single comprehensive work. From the adventures of "The Pioneers of France" a consecutive story is developed through "The Jesuits in North America" and "The Discovery of the Great

West." In "The Old Régime in Canada" it is continued with a masterly analysis of French methods of colonization in this their greatest colony, and then from "Frontenac and New France under Louis XIV." we are led through "A Half-Century of Conflict" to the grand climax in the volumes on "Montcalm and Wolfe," after which "The Conspiracy of Pontiac" brings the long narrative to a noble and brilliant close. In the first volume we see the men of the Stone Age at that brief moment when they were disposed to adore the bearded new-comers as Children of the Sun; in the last we read the bloody story of their last and most desperate, concerted effort to loosen the iron grasp with which these pale-faces had seized and were holding the continent. It is a well-rounded tale, and as complete as anything in real history, where completeness and finality are things unknown.

Between the beginning and end of this well-rounded tale a mighty drama is wrought out in all its scenes. The struggle between France and England for the soil of North America was one of the great critical moments in the career of mankind, — no less important than the struggle between Greece and Persia, or between Rome and Carthage. Out of the long and complicated

interaction between Roman and Teutonic institutions which made up the history of the Middle
Ages, two strongly contrasted forms of political
society had grown up and acquired aggressive
strength when in the course of the sixteenth century a New World beyond the sea was laid
open for colonization.   The maritime nations of
Europe were naturally the ones to be attracted to
this new arena of enterprise ; and Spain, Portugal, France, England, and Holland each played
its interesting and characteristic part.   Spain at
first claimed the whole, excepting only that Bra-
zilian coast which Borgia's decree gave to Portugal.   But Spain's methods, as well as her early
failure of strength, prevented her from making
good her claim.   Spain's methods were limited
to stepping into the place formerly occupied by
the conquering races of half-civilized Indians.
She made aboriginal tribes work for her, just as
the Aztec Confederacy and the Inca dynasty had
done.   Where she was brought into direct contact with American barbarism without the inter-
mediation of half-civilized native races, she made
little or no headway.   Her early failure of
strength, on the other hand, was due to her total
absorption in the fight against civil and religious
liberty in Europe.   The failure became apparent

as soon as the absorption had begun to be complete.   Spain's last aggressive effort in the New World was the destruction of the little Huguenot colony in Florida in 1565, and it is at that point that Parkman's great work appropriately begins.   From that moment Spain simply beat her strength to pieces against the rocks of Netherland courage and resourcefulness.   As for the Netherlands, their energies were so far absorbed in taking over and managing the great Eastern empire of the Portuguese that their work in the New World was confined to seizing upon the most imperial geographical position and planting a cosmopolitan colony there that in the absence of adequate support was sure to fall into the hands of one or the other of the competitors more actively engaged upon the scene.

The two competitors thus more actively engaged were France and England, and from an early period it was felt between the two to be a combat in which no quarter was to be given or accepted.   These two strongly contrasted forms of political society had each its distinct ideal, and that ideal was to be made to prevail, to the utter exclusion and destruction of the other. Probably the French perceived this somewhat

earlier than the English; they felt it to be
necessary to stamp out the English before the
latter had more than realized the necessity of
defending themselves against the French. For
the type of political society represented by
Louis XIV. was pre-eminently militant, as the
English type was pre-eminently industrial. The
aggressiveness of the former was more distinctly
conscious of its own narrower aims, and was
more deliberately set at work to attain them,
while the English, on the other hand, rather
drifted into a tremendous world-fight without
distinct consciousness of their purpose. Yet
after the final issue had been joined, the refrain
Carthago delenda est was heard from the English
side, and it came fraught with impending doom
from the lips of Pitt as in days of old from the
lips of Cato.

The French idea, had it prevailed in the
strife, would not have been capable of building
up a pacific union of partially independent
states, covering this vast continent from ocean
to ocean. Within that rigid and rigorous
bureaucratic system, there was no room for
spontaneous individuality, no room for local
self-government, and no chance for a flexible
federalism to grow up. A well-known phrase

of Louis XIV. was "The state is myself." That phrase represented his ideal. It was approximately true in Old France, realized as far as sundry adverse conditions would allow. The Grand Monarch intended that in New France it should be absolutely true. Upon that fresh soil was to be built up a pure monarchy without concession to human weaknesses and limitations. It was a pet scheme of Louis XIV., and never did a philanthropic world-mender contemplate his grotesque phalanstery or pantarchy with greater pleasure than this master of kingcraft looked forward to the construction of a perfect Christian state in America.

The pages of our great historian are full of examples which prove that if the French idea failed of realization, and the state it founded was overwhelmed, it was not from any lack of lofty qualities in individual Frenchmen. In all the history of the American continent no names stand higher than some of the French names. For courage, for fortitude and high resolve, for sagacious leadership, statesmanlike wisdom, unswerving integrity, devoted loyalty, for all the qualities which make life heroic, we may learn lessons innumerable from the noble

Frenchmen who throng in Mr. Parkman's pages. The difficulty was not in the individuals, but in the system; not in the units, but in the way they were put together. For while it is true — though many people do not know it — that by no imaginable artifice can you make a society that is better than the human units you put into it, it is also true that nothing is easier than to make a society that is worse than its units. So it was with the colony of New France.

Nowhere can we find a description of despotic government more careful and thoughtful, or more graphic and lifelike, than Parkman has given us in his volume on the Old Régime in Canada. Seldom, too, will one find a book fuller of political wisdom. The author never preaches like Carlyle, nor does he hurl huge generalizations at our heads like Buckle; he simply describes a state of society that has been. But I hardly need say that his description is not — like the Dryasdust descriptions we are sometimes asked to accept as history — a mere mass of pigments flung at random upon a canvas. It is a picture painted with consummate art, and in this instance the art consists in so handling the relations of cause and effect as to make them speak for themselves. These pages are alive with political philosophy, and teem with object lessons of extraordinary value. It would be hard to point to any book where History more fully discharges her high function of gathering friendly lessons of caution from the errors of the past.

Of all the societies that have been composed of European men, probably none was ever so despotically organized as New France, unless it may have been the later Byzantine Empire, which it resembled in the minuteness of elaborate supervision over all the pettiest details of life. In Canada the protective, paternal, socialistic, or nationalistic theory of government — it is the same old cloven hoof, under whatever specious name you introduce it — was more fully carried into operation than in any other community known to history except ancient Peru. No room was left for individual initiative or enterprise. All undertakings were nationalized. Government looked after every man's interests in this world and the next, baptized and schooled him, married him and paid the bride's dowry, gave him a bounty with every child that was born to him, stocked his cupboard with garden seeds and compelled him to plant them, prescribed the

size of his house and the number of horses **and**
cattle he might keep, and the exact percentages
of profit he might be allowed to make, and how
his chimneys should be swept, and how many
servants he might employ, and what theological
doctrines he might believe, and what sort of
bread the bakers might bake, and where goods
might be bought and how much might be paid
for them; and if in a society so well cared for **it**
were possible to find indigent persons, such pau-
pers were duly relieved, from a fund established
by government. Unmitigated benevolence was
the theory of Louis XIV.'s Canadian colony, and
heartless political economy had no place there.
Nor was there any room for free-thinkers; when
the King after 1685 sent out word that no mercy
must be shown to heretics, the governor Denon-
ville, with a pious ejaculation, replied that not
so much as a single heretic could be found in all
Canada.

Such was the community whose career our
historian has delineated with perfect soundness
of judgment and wealth of knowledge. The
fate of this nationalistic experiment, set on
foot by one of the most absolute of monarchs
and fostered by one of the most devoted **and**
powerful of religious organizations, is traced **to**

the operation of causes inherent in its very nature.   The hopeless paralysis, the woful corruption, the intellectual and moral torpor resulting
from the suppression of individualism, are vividly portrayed; yet there is no discursive gen-
eralizing, and from moment to moment the development of the story proceeds from within
itself.   It is the whole national life of New
France that is displayed before us.   Historians
of ordinary calibre exhibit their subject in fragments, or they show us some phases of life and
neglect others.   Some have no eyes save for
events that are startling, such as battles and
sieges; or decorative, such as coronations and
court-balls; others give abundant details of manners and customs; others have their attention
absorbed by economics; others again feel such
interest in the history of ideas as to lose sight of
mere material incidents.   Parkman, on the other
hand, conceives and presents his subject as a
whole.   He forgets nothing, overlooks nothing;
but whether it is a bloody battle, or a theological
pamphlet, or an exploring journey through the
forest, or a code for the discipline of nunneries,
each event grows out of its context as a feature
in the total development that is going on before
our eyes.   It is only the historian who is also

. philosopher and artist that can thus deal in block with the great and complex life of a whole society. The requisite combination is realized only in certain rare and high types of mind, and there has been no more brilliant illustration of it than Parkman's volumes afford.

The struggle between the machine-like socialistic despotism of New France and the free and spontaneous political vitality of New England is one of the most instructive object-lessons with which the experience of mankind has furnished us. The depth of its significance is equalled by the vastness of its consequences. Never did Destiny preside over a more fateful contest; for it determined which kind of political seed should be sown all over the widest and richest political garden-plot left untilled in the world. Free industrial England pitted against despotic militant France for the possession of an ancient continent reserved for this decisive struggle, and dragging into the conflict the belated barbarism of the Stone Age, — such is the wonderful theme which Parkman has treated. When the vividly contrasted modern ideas and personages are set off against the romantic though lurid background of Indian life, the artistic effect becomes simply magnificent. Never has historian grap-

pled with another such epic theme save when
Herodotus told the story of Greece and Persia,
or when Gibbon's pages resounded with the
solemn tread of marshalled hosts through a
thousand years of change.

II.

THE story of Mr. Parkman's life can be briefly
told.   He was born in Boston, in what is now
known as Allston Street, Sept. 16, 1823.   His ancestors had for several generations been honorably
known in Massachusetts.   His great-grandfather,
Rev. Ebenezer Parkman, a graduate of Harvard
in 1741, was minister of the Congregational
church in Westborough for nearly sixty years;
he was a man of learning and eloquence, whose
attention was not all given to Calvinistic theology, for he devoted much of it to the study of
history.   A son of this clergyman at the age of
seventeen served as private in a Massachusetts
regiment in that greatest of modern wars which
was decided on the Heights of Abraham.   How
little did this gallant youth dream of the glory
that was by and by to be shed on the scenes and
characters passing before his eyes by the genius
of one of his own race and name !   Another son
óf Ebenezer Parkman returned to Boston and became a successful merchant engaged in that for-

eign traffic which played so important and liber-
alizing a part in American life in the days before
the Enemy of mankind had invented forty-per-
cent tariffs. The home of this merchant, Samuel
Parkman, on the corner of Green and Chardon
streets, was long famous for its beautiful flower-
garden, indicating perhaps the kind of taste and
skill so conspicuous afterwards in his grandson.
In Samuel the clerical profession skipped one
generation, to be taken up again by his son, Rev.
Francis Parkman, a graduate of Harvard in.
1807, and for many years after 1813 the eminent and beloved pastor of the New North
Church. Dr. Parkman was noted for his public
spirit and benevolence. Bishop Huntington, who
knew him well, says of him: " Every aspect of ·
suffering touched him tenderly. There was no ·
hard spot in his breast. His house was the
centre of countless mercies to various forms of
want; and there were few solicitors of alms,
local or itinerant, and whether for private necessity or public benefactions, that his doors did
not welcome and send away satisfied. . . . For
many years he was widely known and esteemed
for his efficient interest in some of our most conspicuous and useful institutions of philanthropy. ·
Among these may be especially mentioned the

Massachusetts Bible Society, the Society for Propagating the Gospel, the Orphan Asylum, the Humane Society, the Medical Dispensary, the Society for the Relief of Aged and Destitute Clergymen, and the Congregational Charitable Society." He also took an active interest in Harvard University, of which he was an overseer. In 1829 he founded there the professorship of "Pulpit Eloquence and the Pastoral Care," familiarly known as the Parkman Professorship. A pupil and friend of Channing, he was noted among Unitarians for a broadly tolerant disposition. His wealth of practical wisdom was enlivened by touches of mirth, so that it was said that you could not "meet Dr. Parkman in the street and stop a minute to exchange words with him without carrying away with you some phrase or turn of thought so exquisite in its mingled sagacity and humor that it touched the inmost sense of the ludicrous, and made the heart smile as well as the lips." Such was the father of our historian.

Mr. Parkman's mother was a descendant of Rev. John Cotton, one of the most eminent of the leaders in the great Puritan exodus of the seventeenth century. She was the daughter of Nathaniel Hall, of Medford, member of a family which was represented in the convention that framed the Constitution of Massachusetts in 1780. Caroline Hall was a lady of remarkable character, and many of her fine qualities were noticeable in her distinguished son. Of her the late Octavius Frothingham says : " Humility, charity, truthfulness, were her prime characteristics. Her conscience was firm and lofty, though never austere. She had a strong sense of right, coupled with perfect charity toward other people; inflexible in principle, she was gentle in practice. Intellectually she could hardly be called brilliant or accomplished, but she had a strong vein of common-sense and practical wisdom, great penetration into character, and a good deal of quiet humor."

Of her six children, the historian, Francis Parkman, was the eldest. As a boy his health was delicate. In a fragment of autobiography, written in the third person, he tells us that "his childhood was neither healthful nor buoyant," and "his boyhood, though for a time active, was not robust." There was a nervous irritability and impulsiveness which kept driving him into activity more intense than his physical strength was well able to bear. At the same time an inborn instinct of self-control, accompanied, doubtless, by a refined unwillingness to intrude his personal feelings upon the notice of other people, led him into such habits of self-repression that his friends sometimes felicitated him on "having no nerves." There was something rudely stoical in his discipline. As he says: "It was impossible that conditions of the nervous system abnormal as his had been from infancy should be without their effects on the mind, and some of these were of a nature highly to exasperate him. Unconscious of their character and origin, and ignorant that with time and confirmed health they would have disappeared, he had no other thought than that of crushing them by force, and accordingly applied himself to the work. Hence resulted a state of mental tension, habitual for several years, and abundantly mischievous in its effects. With a mind overstrained and a body overtasked, he was burning his candle at both ends."

The conditions which were provided for the sensitive and highly strung boy during a part of his childhood were surely very delightful, and there can be little doubt that they served to determine his career. His grandfather Hall's home in Medford was situated on the border of

the Middlesex Fells, a rough and rocky woodland, four thousand acres in extent, as wild and
savage in many places as any primeval forest.
The place is within eight miles of Boston, and
it may be doubted if anywhere else can be found
another such magnificent piece of wilderness so
near to a great city. It needs only a stray Indian or two, with a few bears and wolves, to
bring back for us the days when Winthrop's
company landed on the shores of the neighboring bay. In the heart of this shaggy woodland
is Spot Pond, a lake of glorious beauty, with a
surface of three hundred acres, and a homely
name which it is to be hoped it may always
keep, — a name bestowed in the good old times
before the national vice of magniloquence had
begun to deface our maps. Among the pleasure
drives in the neighborhood of Boston, the drive
around Spot Pond is perhaps foremost in beauty.
A few fine houses have been built upon its borders, and well-kept roads have given to some
parts of the forest the aspect of a park, but the
greater part of the territory is undisturbed and
will probably remain so. Seventy years ago the
pruning hand of civilization had scarcely touched
it. To his grandfather's farm, on the outskirts
of this enchanting spot, the boy Parkman was sent

in his eighth year. There, he tells us, "I walked twice a day to a school of high but undeserved reputation, about a mile distant in the town of Medford. Here I learned very little, and spent the intervals of schooling more profitably in collecting eggs, insects, and reptiles, trapping squirrels and woodchucks, and making persistent though rarely fortunate attempts to kill birds with arrows. After four years of this rustication I was brought back to Boston, when I was unhappily seized with a mania for experiments in chemistry, involving a lonely, confined, unwholesome sort of life, baneful to body and mind." No doubt the experience of four years of plastic boyhood in Middlesex Fells gave to Parkman's mind the bent which directed him towards the history of the wilderness. This fact he recognized of himself in after life, while he recalled those boyish days as the brightest in his memory.

At the age of fifteen or so the retorts and crucibles were thrown away forever, and a reaction in favor of woodland life began; "a fancy," he says, "which soon gained full control over the course of the literary pursuits to which he was also addicted." Here we come upon the first mention of the combination of interests which determined his career. A million boys might be turned loose in Middlesex Fells, one after another, there to roam in solitude until our globe should have entered upon a new geological period, and the chances are against any one of them becoming a great historian, or anything else above mediocrity. But in Parkman, as in all men of genius, the dominant motive-power was something within him, something which science has not data enough to explain. The divine spark of genius is something which we know only through the acts which it excites. In Parkman the strong literary instinct showed itself at Chauncy Hall School, where we find him at fourteen years of age eagerly and busily engaged in the study and practice of English composition. It was natural that tales of heroes should be especially charming at that time of life, and among Parkman's efforts were paraphrasing parts of the "Æneid," and turning into rhymed verse the scene of the tournament in "Ivanhoe." From the artificial stupidity which is too often superinduced in boys by their early schooling, he was saved by native genius and breezy woodland life, and his progress was rapid. In 1840, having nearly completed his seventeenth year, he entered Harvard College. His reputation there for scholarship was good; but he was much more absorbed in his own pursuits than in the regular college studies. In the summer vacation of 1841, he made a rough journey of exploration in the woods of northern New Hampshire, accompanied by one classmate and a native guide, and there he had a taste of adventure slightly spiced with hardship.

How much importance this ramble may have had, one cannot say, but he tells us that " before the end of the Sophomore year my various schemes had crystallized into a plan of writing the story of what was then known as the ' Old French War,' — that is, the war that ended in the conquest of Canada, — for here, as it seemed to me, the forest drama was more stirring, and the forest stage more thronged with appropriate actors than in any other passage of our history. It was not until some years later that I enlarged the plan to include the whole course of the American conflict between France and England, or, in other words, the history of the American forest; for this was the light in which I regarded it. My theme fascinated me, and I was haunted with wilderness images day and night." The way in which true genius works could not be more happily described.

When the great scheme first took shape in Mr. Parkman's mind, he reckoned that it would take about twenty years to complete the task. How he entered upon it may best be told in his own words. "The time allowed was ample; but here he fell into a fatal error, entering on this long pilgrimage with all the vehemence of one starting on a mile heat. His reliance, however, was less on books than on such personal experience as should in some sense identify him with his theme. His natural inclinations urged him in the same direction, for his thoughts were always in the forest, whose features, not unmixed with softer images, possessed his waking and sleeping dreams, filling him with vague cravings impossible to satisfy. As fond of hardships as he was vain of enduring them, cherishing a sovereign scorn for every physical weakness or defect, deceived moreover by a rapid development of frame and sinews which flattered him with the belief that discipline sufficiently unsparing would harden him into an athlete, he slighted the precautions of a more reasonable woodcraft, tired old foresters with long marches, stopped neither for heat nor rain, and slept on the earth without a blanket." In other words, "a highly irritable organism spurred the writer to excess in a course which, with one of different temperament, would have produced a free and hardy development of such faculties and forces as he possessed." Along with the irritable organism perhaps a heritage of fierce ancestral Puritanism may have prompted him to the stoical discipline which sought to ignore the just claims of the physical body. He tells us of his undoubting faith that "to tame the Devil, it is best to take him by the horns;" but more mature experiences made him feel less sure "of the advantages of this method of dealing with that subtle personage."

Under these conditions perhaps the college vacations which he spent in the woods of Canada and New England may have done more to exhaust than to recruit his strength. In his junior year some physical injury, the nature of which does not seem to be known, caused it to be thought necessary to send him to Europe for his health. He went first to Gibraltar in a sailing ship, and a passage from his diary may serve to throw light upon the voyage and the man: " It was a noble sight when at intervals the sun broke out over the savage waves, changing their blackness to a rich blue almost as dark; while the foam that flew over it seemed like whirling snow wreaths on the mountain. . . . As soon as it was daybreak I went on deck. Two or three sails were set. The vessel scouring along, leaning over so that her lee gunwale scooped up the water ; the water in a foam, and clouds of spray flying over us, frequently as high as the main yard. The spray was driven with such force that it pricked the cheek like needles. I stayed on deck two or three hours, when, being thoroughly salted, I went down, changed my clothes, and read ' Don Quixote ' till Mr. Snow appeared at the door with ' You are the man that wants to see a gale, are ye ? Now is your chance ; only just come up on deck.' Accordingly I went. The wind was yelling and howling in the rigging in a fashion that reminded me of a storm in a Canadian forest. . . . The sailors clung, half-drowned, to whatever they could lay hold of, for the vessel was at times half inverted, and tons of water washed from side to side of her deck."

Mr. Parkman's route was from Gibraltar by way of Malta, to Sicily, where he travelled over the whole island, and thence to Naples, where he fell in with the great preacher, Theodore Parker. Together they climbed Vesuvius and peered into its crater, and afterwards in and about Rome they renewed their comradeship. Here Mr. Parkman wished to spend a few weeks in a monastery, in order to study with his own eyes the priests and their way of life. More than once he met with a prompt and uncompromising refusal, but at length the coveted privilege was granted him ; and, curiously enough, it was by the strictest of all the monastic orders, the Passionists, brethren addicted to wearing hair shirts and scourging themselves without mercy. When these worthy monks learned that their visitor was not merely a Protestant but a Unitarian, their horror was intense ; but they were ready for the occasion, poor souls ! and tried their best to convert him, thereby doubtless enhancing their value in the historian's eyes as living and breathing historic material. This visit was surely of inestimable service to the pen which was to be so largely occupied with the Jesuits and Franciscans of the New World.

Mr. Parkman did not leave Rome until he had seen temples, churches, and catacombs, and had been presented to the Pope. He stopped at Florence, Bologna, Modena, Parma, and Milan, and admired the Lake of Como, to which, how-ever, he preferred the savage wildness of Lake

George. He saw something of Switzerland, went to Paris and London, and did a bit of sight-seeing in Edinburgh and its neighborhood. From Liverpool he sailed for America; and in spite of the time consumed in this trip we find him taking his degree at Cambridge, along with his class, in 1844. Probably his name stood high in the rank list, for he was at once elected a member of the Phi Beta Kappa Society. After this he entered the Law School, but stayed not long, for his life's work was already claiming him. In his brief vacation journeys he had seen tiny remnants of wilderness here and there in Canada or in lonely corners of New England; now he wished to see the wilderness itself in all its gloom and vastness, and to meet face to face with the dusky warriors of the Stone Age. At this end of the nineteenth century, as already observed, such a thing can no longer be done. Nowhere now, within the United States, does the primitive wilderness exist, save here and there in shreds and patches. In the middle of the century it covered the western half of the continent, and could be reached by a journey of sixteen or seventeen hundred miles, from Boston to the plains of Nebraska. Parkman had become an adept in woodcraft and a dead

·shot with the rifle, and could do such things
. with horses, tame or wild, as civilized people
• never see done except in a circus. There was
. little doubt as to his ability to win the respect
of Indians by outshining them in such deeds
as they could appreciate. Early in 1846 he
• started for the wilderness with Mr. Quincy
Shaw. A passage from the preface to the
fourth edition of " The Oregon Trail," published
in 1872, will here be of interest : —

" I remember as we rode by the foot of Pike's
Peak, when for a fortnight we met no face of
man, my companion remarked, in a tone any-
-thing but complacent, that a time would come
when those plains would be a grazing country,
the buffalo give place to tame cattle, houses be
scattered along the water-courses, and wolves,
bears, and Indians be numbered among the
things that were. We condoled with each other
on so melancholy a prospect, but with little
thought what the future had in store. We
knew that there was more or less gold in the
seams of those untrodden mountains; but we
did not foresee that it would build cities in
the West, and plant hotels and gambling-houses
among the haunts of the grizzly bear. We knew
. that a few fanatical outcasts were groping their

way across the plains to seek an asylum from
Gentile persecution; but we did not imagine
that the polygamous hordes of Mormons would
rear a swarming Jerusalem in the bosom of solitude itself. We knew that more and more, year
after year, the trains of emigrant wagons would
creep in slow procession towards barbarous
Oregon or wild and distant California; but we
did not dream how Commerce and Gold would
breed nations along the Pacific; the disenchant-
ing screech of the locomotive break the spell
of weird, mysterious mountains; woman's rights
invade the fastnesses of the Arapahoes; and
despairing savagery, assailed in front and rear, `
veil its scalp-locks and feathers before triumphant commonplace. We were no prophets to .
foresee all this; and had we foreseen it, perhaps ·
some perverse regret might have tempered the
ardor of our rejoicing.

"The wild tribe that defiled with me down
the gorges of the Black Hills, with its paint and
war-plumes, fluttering trophies and savage em-
broidery, bows, arrows, lances, and shields, will
never be seen again. Those who formed it have
found bloody graves, or a ghastlier burial in the
maws of wolves. The Indian of to-day, armed
with a revolver and crowned with an old hat,

cased, possibly, in trousers, or muffled in a tawdry shirt, is an Indian still, but an Indian shorn of the picturesqueness which was his most conspicuous merit. The mountain trapper is no more, and the grim romance of his wild, hard life is a memory of the past."

This first of Parkman's books, "The Oregon Trail," was published in 1847, as a series of articles in the "Knickerbocker Magazine." Its pages reveal such supreme courage, such physical hardiness, such rapturous enjoyment of life, that one finds it hard to realize that even in setting out upon this bold expedition the writer was something of an invalid. A weakness of sight — whether caused by some direct injury, or a result of widespread nervous disturbance, is not quite clear — had already become serious and somewhat alarming. On arriving at the Indian camp, near the Medicine Bow range of the Rocky Mountains, he was suffering from a complication of disorders. "I was so reduced by illness," he says, "that I could seldom walk without reeling like a drunken man, and when I rose from my seat upon the ground the landscape suddenly grew dim before my eyes, the trees and lodges seemed to sway to and fro, and the prairie to rise and fall like the

swells of the ocean. Such a state of things is
not enviable anywhere. In a country where a
man's life may at any moment depend on the
strength of his arm, or it may be on the activity
of his legs, it is more particularly inconvenient.
Nor is sleeping on damp ground, with an occasional drenching from a shower, very beneficial
in such cases. I sometimes suffered the extremity of exhaustion, and was in a tolerably
fair way of atoning for my love of the prairie
by resting there forever. I tried repose and a
very sparing diet. For a long time, with exem-
plary patience, I lounged about the camp, or at
the utmost staggered over to the Indian village,
and walked faint and dizzy among the lodges.
It would not do, and I bethought me of starvation. During five days I sustained life on one
small biscuit a day. At the end of that time I
was weaker than before, but the disorder seemed
shaken in its stronghold, and very gradually I
began to resume a less rigid diet." It did not
seem prudent to Parkman to let the signs of
physical ailment become conspicuous, " since in
that case a horse, a rifle, a pair of pistols, and
a red shirt might have offered temptations too
strong for aboriginal virtue." Therefore, in
order that his prestige with the red men might

not suffer diminution, he would "hunt buffalo
on horseback over a broken country, when without the tonic of the chase he could scarcely sit
upright in the saddle."

The maintenance of prestige was certainly
desirable. The Ogillalah band of Sioux, among
whom he found himself, were thorough savages.
"Neither their manners nor their ideas were in
the slightest degree modified by contact with civilization. They knew nothing of the power and
real character of the white men, and their children
would scream in terror when they saw me. Their
religion, superstitions, and prejudices were the
same handed down to them from immemorial
time. They fought with the weapons that their
fathers fought with, and wore the same garments
of skins. They were living representatives of the
Stone Age; for though their lances and arrows
were tipped with iron procured from the traders,
they still used the rude stone mallet of the primeval world." These savages welcomed Parkman
and one of his white guides with cordial hospitality, and they were entertained by the chieftain
Big Crow, whose lodge in the evening presented
a picturesque spectacle. "A score or more of
Indians were seated around it in a circle, their
dark, naked forms just visible by the dull light

of the smouldering fire in the middle. The pipe
glowed brightly in the gloom as it passed from
hand to hand. Then a squaw would drop a
piece of buffalo-fat on the dull embers. Instantly a bright flame would leap up, darting
its light to the very apex of the tall conical
structure, where the tops of the slender poles
that supported the covering of hide were gathered together. It gilded the features of the
Indians, as with animated gestures they sat
around it, telling their endless stories of war
and hunting, and displayed rude garments of
skins that hung around the lodge; the bow,
quiver, and lance suspended over the resting-
place of the chief, and the rifles and powder-
horns of the two white guests. For a moment
all would be bright as day; then the flames
would die out; fitful flashes from the embers
would illumine the lodge, and then leave it in
darkness. Then the light would wholly fade,
and the lodge and all within it be involved
again in obscurity." From stories of war and
the chase, the conversation was now and then
diverted to philosophic themes. When Parkman
asked what makes the thunder, various opinions
were expressed; but one old wrinkled fellow,
named Red Water, asseverated that he had

always known what it was. " It was a great black bird; and once he had seen it in a dream swooping down from the Black Hills, with its loud roaring wings; and when it flapped them over a lake, they struck lightning from the water." Another old man said that the wicked thunder had killed his brother last summer, but doggedly refused to give any particulars. It was afterwards learned that this brother was member of a thunder-fighting fraternity of priests or medicine-men. On the approach of a storm they would " take their bows and arrows, their magic drum, and a sort of whistle made out of the wing-bone of the war-eagle, and, thus equipped, run out and fire at the rising cloud, whooping, yelling, whistling, and beating their drum to frighten it down again. One afternoon a heavy black cloud was coming up, and they repaired to the top of a hill, where they brought all their magic artillery into play against it. But the undaunted thunder, refusing to be ter- rified, darted out a bright flash, which struck [the aforesaid brother] dead as he was in the very act of shaking his long iron-pointed lance against it. The rest scattered and ran yelling in an ecstasy of superstitious terror back to their lodges."

One should read Mr. Parkman's detailed narrative of the strange life of these people, and the manner of his taking part in it; how he called the villagers together and regaled them sumptuously with boiled dog, and made them a skilful speech, in which he quite satisfied them as to his reasons for coming to dwell among them; how a warm friendship grew up between himself and the venerable Red Water, who was the custodian of an immense fund of folk-lore, but was apt to be superstitiously afraid of imparting any of it to strangers; how war-parties were projected and abandoned, how buffalo and antelope were hunted, and how life was carried on in the dull intervals between such occupations. If one were to keep on quoting what is of especial interest in the book, one would have to quote the whole of it. But one characteristic portrait contains so much insight into Indian life that I cannot forbear giving it. It is the sketch of the young fellow called the Hail-Storm, as Parkman found him one evening on the return from the chase, "his light graceful figure reclining on the ground in an easy attitude, while . . . near him lay the fresh skin of a female elk, which he had just killed among the mountains, only a mile or two from camp. No doubt the boy's heart was elated with triumph, but he betrayed no sign of it. He even seemed totally unconscious of our approach, and his handsome face had all the tranquillity of Indian self-control, — a self-control which prevents the exhibition of emotion without restraining the emotion itself. It was about two months since I had known the Hail-Storm, and within that time his character had remarkably developed. When I first saw him, he was just emerging from the habits and feelings of the boy into the ambition of the hunter and warrior. He had lately killed his first deer, and this had excited his aspirations for distinction. Since that time he had been continually in search for game, and no young hunter in the village had been so active or so fortunate as he. All this success had produced a marked change in his character. As I first remembered him he always shunned the society of the young squaws, and was extremely bashful and sheepish in their presence ; but now, in the confidence of his new reputation, he began to assume the airs and arts of a man of gallantry. He wore his red blanket dashingly over his left shoulder, painted his cheeks every day with vermilion, and hung pendants of shells in his ears. If I observed aright, he met with very good success in his new pursuits; still the Hail-Storm had much to accomplish before he attained the full standing of a warrior. Gallantly as he began to bear himself before the women and girls, he was still timid and abashed in the presence of the chiefs and old men; for he had never yet killed a man, or stricken the dead body of an enemy in battle. I have no doubt that the handsome smooth-faced boy burned with desire to flesh his maiden scalping-knife, and I would not have encamped alone with him without watching his movements with a suspicious eye." Mr. Parkman once told me that it was rare for a young brave to obtain full favor with the women without having at least one scalp to show; and this fact was one of the secret sources of danger which the ordinary white visitor would never think of. Peril is also liable to lurk in allowing oneself to be placed in a ludicrous light among these people; accordingly, whenever such occasions arose, Parkman knew enough to " maintain a rigid inflexible countenance, and [thus] wholly escaped their sallies." He understood that his rifle and pistols were the only friends on whom he could invariably rely when alone among Indians. His own observation taught him "the extreme folly of confidence, and the utter impossibility of fore-

e

seeing to what sudden acts the strange unbridled impulses of an Indian may urge him. When among this people danger is never so near as when you are unprepared for it, never so remote as when you are armed and on the alert to meet it at any moment. Nothing offers so strong a temptation to their ferocious instincts as the appearance of timidity, weakness, or security."

The immense importance of this sojourn in the wilderness, in its relation to Parkman's life-work, is obvious. Knowledge, intrepidity, and tact carried him through it unscathed, and good luck kept him clear of encounters with hostile Indians, in which these qualities might not have sufficed to avert destruction. It was rare good fortune that kept his party from meeting with an enemy during five months of travel through a dangerous region. Scarcely three weeks after he had reached the confines of civilization, the Pawnees and Comanches began a systematized series of hostilities, and "attacked . . . every party, large or small, that passed during the next six months."

During this adventurous experience, says Parkman, "my business was observation, and I was willing to pay dearly for the opportunity of exercising it." A heavy price was exacted of him, not by red men, but by that "subtle person-age" whom he had tried to take by the horns, and who seems to have resented such presumption. Towards the end of the journey Parkman found himself ill in much the same way as at the beginning, and craved medical advice. It was in mid September, on a broad meadow in the wild valley of the Arkansas, where his party had fallen in with a huge Santa Fé caravan of white-topped wagons, with great droves of mules and horses; and we may let Parkman tell the story in his own words, in the last of our extracts from his fascinating book. One of the guides had told him that in this caravan was a physician from St. Louis, by the name of Dobbs, of the very highest standing in his profession. "Without at all believing him, I resolved to consult this eminent practitioner. Walking over to the camp, I found him lying sound asleep under one of the wagons. He offered in his own person but indifferent evidence of his skill; for it was five months since I had seen so cadaverous a face. His hat had fallen off, and his yellow hair was all in disorder; one of his arms supplied the place of a pillow; his trousers were wrinkled halfway up to his knees, and he was covered with little bits of grass and straw upon which he had rolled in his uneasy slumber. A Mexican stood near, and I made him a sign to touch the doctor. Up sprang the learned Dobbs, and sitting upright rubbed his eyes and looked about him in bewilderment. I regretted the necessity of disturbing him, and said I had come to ask professional advice.

"'Your system, sir, is in a disordered state,' said he, solemnly, after a short examination. I inquired what might be the particular species of disorder. 'Evidently a morbid action of the liver,' replied the medical man; 'I will give you a prescription.'

"Repairing to the back of one of the covered wagons, he scrambled in; for a moment I could see nothing of him but his boots. At length he produced a box which he had extracted from some dark recess within, and opening it presented me with a folded paper. 'What is it,' said I. 'Calomel,' said the doctor.

"Under the circumstances I would have taken almost anything. There was not enough to do me much harm, and it might possibly do good; so at camp that night I took the poison instead of supper."

After the return from the wilderness Mr.

Parkman found his physical condition rather worse than better. The trouble with the eyes continued, and we begin to find mention of a lameness which was sometimes serious enough to confine him to the house, and which seems to have lasted a long time; but from this he seems to have recovered. My personal acquaintance with him began in 1872, and I never noticed any symptoms of lameness, though I remember taking several pleasant walks with him. Perhaps the source of the lameness may be indicated in the following account of his condition in 1848, cited from the fragment of autobiography in which he uses the third person: " To the maladies of the prairie succeeded a suite of exhausting disorders, so reducing him that circulation of the extremities ceased, the light of the sun became insupportable, and a wild whirl possessed his brain, joined to a universal turmoil of the nervous system which put his philosophy to the sharpest test it had hitherto known. All collapsed, in short, but the tenacious strength of muscles hardened by long activity." In 1851, whether due or not to disordered circulation, there came an effusion of water on the left knee, which for the next two years prevented walking.

It was between 1848 and 1851 that Mr. Parkman was engaged in writing "The Conspiracy of
Pontiac." He felt that no regimen could be
worse for him than idleness, and that no tonic
could be more bracing than work in pursuance
of the lofty purpose which had now attained
maturity in his mind. He had to contend with
a "triple-headed monster": first, the weakness
of the eyes, which had come to be such that he
could not keep them open to the light while
writing his own name; secondly, the incapacity
for sustained attention; and thirdly, the indis-
position to putting forth mental effort. Evidently the true name of this triple-headed monster was nervous exhaustion; there was too
much soul for the body to which it was yoked.

" To be made with impunity, the attempt
must be made with the most watchful caution.
He caused a wooden frame to be constructed of
the size and shape of a sheet of letter-paper.
Stout wires were fixed horizontally across it, half
an inch apart, and a movable back of thick
pasteboard fitted behind them. The paper for
writing was placed between the pasteboard
and the wires, guided by which, and using a
black lead crayon, he could write not illegibly
with closed eyes. He was at the time absent

from home, on Staten Island, where, and in the neighboring city of New York, he had friends who willingly offered their aid. It is needless to say to which half of humanity nearly all these kind assistants belonged. He chose for a beginning that part of the work which offered fewest difficulties and with the subject of which he was most familiar; namely, the Siege of Detroit. The books and documents, already partially arranged, were procured from Boston, and read to him at such times as he could listen to them, the length of each reading never without injury much exceeding half an hour, and periods of several days frequently occurring during which he could not listen at all. Notes were made by him with closed eyes, and afterwards deciphered and read to him till he had mastered them. For the first half-year the rate of composition averaged about six lines a day. The portion of the book thus composed was afterwards partially rewritten.

"His health improved under the process, and the remainder of the volume — in other words, nearly the whole of it — was composed in Boston, while pacing in the twilight of a large garret, the only exercise which the sensitive condition of his sight permitted him in an unclouded

day while the sun was above the horizon. It
was afterwards written down from dictation by
relatives under the same roof, to whom he was
also indebted for the preparatory readings. His
progress was much less tedious than at the outset, and the history was complete in about two
years and a half."

The book composed under such formidable
difficulties was published in 1851. It did not at
once meet with the reception which it deserved.
The reading public did not expect to find entertainment in American history. In the New
England of those days the general reader had
heard a good deal about the Pilgrim Fathers
and Salem Witchcraft and remembered hazily the
stories of Hannah Dustin and of Putnam and
the wolf, but could not be counted on for much
else before the Revolution. I remember once
hearing it said that the story of the " Old
French War " was something of no more interest or value for Americans of to-day than the
cuneiform records of an insurrection in ancient
Nineveh ; and so slow are people in gaining a
correct historical perspective that within the last
ten years the mighty world-struggle in which
Pitt and Frederick were allied is treated in a
book entitled " Minor Wars of the United

States"! In 1851 the soil was not yet ready
for the seed sown by Parkman, and he did not
quickly or suddenly become popular. But after
the publication of the "Pioneers of France" in
1865 his fame grew rapidly. In those days I
took especial pleasure in praising his books, from
the feeling that they were not so generally
known as they ought to be, particularly in England, where he has since come to be recognized
as foremost among American writers of history.
In 1879 I had been giving a course of lectures
at University College, London, on "America's
Place in History," and shortly afterwards repeated this course at the little Hawthorne Hall,
on Park Street, in Boston. One evening, having
occasion to allude briefly to Pontiac and his conspiracy, I said, among other things, that it was
memorable as "the theme of one of the most
brilliant and fascinating books that has ever
been written by any historian since the days
of Herodotus." The words were scarcely out of
my mouth when I happened to catch sight of
Mr. Parkman in my audience. I had not observed him before, though he was seated quite
near me. I shall never forget the sudden start
which he gave, and the heightened color of his
noble face, with its curious look of surprise and

pleasure, an expression as honest and simple as one might witness in a rather shy schoolboy suddenly singled out for praise. I was so glad that I had said what I did without thinking of his hearing me.

In May, 1850, while at work upon this great book, Mr. Parkman married Catherine, daughter of Jacob Bigelow, an eminent physician of Boston. Of this marriage there were three children, — a son, who died while an infant, and two daughters, who still survive. Mrs. Parkman died in 1858, and her husband never married again.

During these years, when his complicated ailments for a time made historical work impossible, even to this man of Titanic will, he assuaged his cravings for spiritual creation by writing a novel, "Vassall Morton." Of his books it is the only one that I have never seen, and I can speak of it only from hearsay. It is said to be not without signal merits, but it did not find a great many readers, and its author seems not to have cared much for it. The main current of his interest in life was too strong to allow of much diversion into side channels.

"Meanwhile," to cite his own words, "the Faculty of Medicine were not idle, displaying that exuberance of resource for which that remarkable profession is justly famed. The wisest, indeed, did nothing, commending his patient to time and faith; but the activity of his brethren made full amends for this masterly inaction. One was for tonics, another for a diet of milk; one counselled galvanism, another hydropathy; one scarred him behind the neck with nitric acid, another drew red-hot irons along his spine with a view of enlivening that organ. Opinion was divergent as practice. One assured him of recovery in six years; another thought that he would never recover. Another, with grave circumlocution, lest the patient should take fright, informed him that he was the victim of an organic disease of the brain which must needs despatch him to another world within a twelvemonth; and he stood amazed at the smile of an auditor who neither cared for the announcement nor believed it. Another, an eminent physiologist of Paris, after an acquaintance of three months, one day told him that from the nature of the disorder he had at first supposed that it must, in accordance with precedent, be attended with insanity, and had ever since been studying him to discover under what form the supposed aberration de-

clared itself, adding, with a somewhat humorous
look, that his researches had not been rewarded
with the smallest success."

Soon after his marriage, Mr. Parkman became
possessor of a small estate of three acres or so
in Jamaica Plain, on the steep shore of the
beautiful pond. It was a charming place, thoroughly English in its homelike simplicity and
refined comfort. The house stood near the
entrance, and on not far from the same level
as the roadway; but from the side and rear the
ground fell off rapidly, so that it was quite a
sharp descent to the pretty little wharf or dock,
where one might sit and gaze on the placid,
dreamy water. It is with that lovely home that
Mr. Parkman is chiefly associated in my mind.
Twenty years ago, while I was acting as librarian at Harvard University, he was a member of
the corporation, and I had frequent occasion to
consult with him on matters of business. At
such times I would drive over from Cambridge
or take a street-car to Jamaica Plain, sure of a
cordial greeting and a pleasant chat, in which
business always received its full measure of
justice, and was then thrust aside for more inspiring themes. The memory of one day in
particular will go with me through life, — an

enchanted day in the season of apple-blossoms,
when I went in the morning for a brief errand,
taking with me one of my little sons. The brief
errand ended in spending the whole day and
staying until late in the evening, while the
world of thought was ransacked and some of
its weightiest questions provisionally settled!
Nor was either greenhouse or garden or pond
neglected. At such times there was nothing in
Mr. Parkman's looks or manner to suggest the
invalid. He and I were members of a small
club of a dozen or more congenial spirits who
now for nearly thirty years have met once a
month to dine together. When he came to the
dinner he was always one of the most charming
companions at the table, but ill health often
prevented his coming, and in the latter years
of his life he never came. I knew nothing of
the serious nature of his troubles; and when I
heard the cause of his absence alleged, I used
to suppose that it was merely some need for
taking care of digestion or avoiding late hours
that kept him at home. What most impressed
one, in talking with him, was the combination
of power and alertness with extreme gentleness.
Nervous irritability was the last thing of which
I should have suspected him. He never made

the slightest allusion to his ill health; he would probably have deemed it inconsistent with good breeding to intrude upon his friends with such topics; and his appearance was always most cheerful. His friend (our common friend), the late Octavius Frothingham, says of him: "Again and again he had to restrain the impulse to say vehement things, or to do violent deeds without the least provocation; but he maintained so absolutely his moral self-control that none but the closest observer would notice any deviation from the most perfect calm and serenity." I can testify that until after Mr. Parkman's death I had never dreamed of the existence of any such deviation.

Garden and greenhouse formed a very important part of the home by Jamaica Pond. Mr. Parkman's love for Nature was in no way more conspicuously shown than in his diligence and skill in cultivating flowers. It is often observed that plants will grow for some persons, but not for others; one man's conservatory will be heavy with verdure, gorgeous in its colors, and redolent of sweet odors, while his neighbor's can show nothing but a forlorn assemblage of pots and sticks. The difference is due to the loving care which learns and humors the idiosyncrasies of each individual thing that grows; the keen observation of the naturalist supplemented by the watchful solicitude of the nurse. Among the indications of rare love and knowledge of Nature is marked success in inducing her to bring forth her most exquisite creations, the flowers. As an expert in horticulture Mr. Parkman achieved celebrity. His garden and greenhouse had extraordinary things to show. As he pointed out to me on my first visit to them, he followed Darwinian methods and originated new varieties of plants. The *Lilium Parkmani* has long been famous among florists. He was also eminent in the culture of roses, and author of a work entitled " The Book of Roses," which was published in 1866. He was President of the Horticultural Society, and at one time Professor of Horticulture in Harvard University. There can be no doubt as to the beneficial effects of these pursuits. It is wholesome to be out of doors with spade and trowel and sprinkler; there is something tonic in the aroma of fresh damp loam; and nothing is more restful to the soul than daily sympathetic intercourse with flowering plants. It was surely here that Mr. Parkman found his best medicine.

When he entered, in 1851, upon his great work on "France and England in the New World," he had before him the task "of tracing out, collecting, indexing, arranging, and digesting a great mass of incongruous material scattered on both sides of the Atlantic." A considerable portion of this material was in manuscript, and involved much tedious exploration and the employment of trained copyists. It was necessary to study carefully the catalogues of many European libraries, and to open correspondence with such scholars and public officials in both hemispheres as might be able to point to the whereabouts of fresh sources of information. Work of this sort, as one bit of clew leads to another, is capable of arousing the emotion of pursuit to a very high degree; and I believe the effect of it upon Mr. Parkman's health must have been good, in spite of, or rather because of, its difficulties. The chase was carried on until his manuscript treasures had been brought to an extraordinary degree of completeness. These made his library quite remarkable. In printed books it was far less rich. He had not the tastes of a bibliophile, and did not feel it necessary, as Freeman did, to own all the books he used. His library of printed books, which at his

death went to Harvard University, was a very
small one for a scholar, — about twenty-five hundred volumes, including more or less of Greek
and Latin literature and theology inherited from
his father.   His manuscripts, as I have already
mentioned, went to the library of the Massachusetts Historical Society.

When the manuscripts had come into his
hands, an arduous labor was begun.   All had to
be read to him and taken in slowly, bit by bit.
The incapacity to keep steadily at work made it
impossible to employ regular assistants profitably ; and for readers he either depended upon
members of his own family or called in pupils
from the public schools.   Once he speaks of having had a well-trained young man, who was an
excellent linguist ; on another occasion it was a
school-girl "ignorant of any tongue but her
own," and "the effect, though highly amusing
to bystanders, was far from being so to the person endeavoring to follow the meaning of this
singular jargon."   The larger part of the documents used in preparing the earlier volumes were
in seventeenth-century French, which, though far
from being Old French, is enough unlike the nine-
teenth-century speech to have troubled Mr. Parkman's readers and thus to have worried his ears.

f

As Mr. Frothingham describes his method, when the manuscripts were slowly read to him, " first the chief points were considered, then the details of the story were gone over carefully and minutely. As the reading went on he made notes, first of essential matters, then of non-essential. After this he welded everything together, made the narrative completely his own, infused into it his own fire, quickened it by his own imagination, and made it, as it were, a living experience, so that his books read like personal reminiscences. It was certainly a slow and painful process, but the result more than justified the labor."

In the fragment of autobiography already quoted, which Mr. Parkman left with Dr. Ellis in 1868, but which was apparently written in 1865, he says: " One year, four years, and numerous short intervals lasting from a day to a month, represent the literary interruptions since the work in hand was begun. Under the most favorable conditions, it was a slow and doubtful navigation, beset with reefs and breakers, demanding a constant lookout and a constant throwing of the lead. Of late years, however, the condition of the sight has so far improved as to permit reading, not exceeding

on the average five minutes at one time. This
modicum of power, though apparently trifling,
proves of the greatest service, since by a cautious
management its application may be extended.
By reading for one minute, and then resting for
an equal time, this alternate process may generally be continued for about half an hour. Then
after a sufficient interval it may be repeated,
often three or four times in the course of the
day. By this means nearly the whole of the
volume now offered [Pioneers] has been composed. . . . How far, by a process combining
the slowness of the tortoise with the uncertainty
of the hare, an undertaking of close and extended research can be advanced, is a question
to solve which there is no aid from precedent,
since it does not appear that an attempt under
similar circumstances has hitherto been made.
The writer looks, however, for a fair degree of
success."

After 1865 the progress was certainly much
more rapid than before. The next fourteen
years witnessed the publication of "The Jesuits,",
"La Salle," "The Old Régime," and "Frontenac," and saw "Montcalm and Wolfe" well
under way; while the "Half-Century of Conflict" intervening between "Frontenac" and

"Montcalm and Wolfe" was reserved until the last-mentioned work should be done, for the same reason that led Herbert Spencer to postpone the completing of his "Sociology" until he should have finished his "Principles of Ethics." In view of life's vicissitudes, it was prudent to make sure of the crowning work at all events, leaving some connecting links to be inserted afterwards. As one obstacle after another was surmounted, as one grand division of the work after another became an accomplished fact, the effect upon Mr. Parkman's condition must have been bracing, and he seems to have acquired fresh impetus as he approached the goal.

For desultory work in the shape of magazine articles he had little leisure; but two essays of his, on "The Failure of Universal Suffrage" and on "The Reasons against Woman Suffrage," are very thoughtful, and worthy of serious consideration. In questions of political philosophy, his conclusions, which were reached from a very wide and impartial survey of essential facts, always seemed to me of the highest value.

When I look back upon Parkman's noble life, I think of Mendelssohn's chorus, "He that shall endure to the end," with its chaste and severely beautiful melody and the calm,

invincible faith which it expresses. After all
the harrowing years of doubt and distress, the
victory was such in its magnitude as has been
granted to but few mortals to win. He lived
to see his life's work done; the thought of his
eighteenth year was realized in his sixty-ninth;
and its greatness had come to be admitted
throughout the civilized world. In September,
1893, his seventieth year was completed, and
his autumn in the lovely home at Jamaica Plain
was a pleasant one. On the first Sunday afternoon in November he rowed on the pond in his
boat, but felt ill as he returned to the house, and
on the next Wednesday, the eighth, he passed
quietly away. Thus he departed from a world
which will evermore be the richer and better
for having once had him as its denizen. The
memory of a life so strong and beautiful is a
precious possession for us all.

As for the book on which he labored with
such marvellous heroism, a word may be said in
conclusion. Great in his natural powers and
great in the use he made of them, Parkman
was no less great in his occasion and in his
theme. Of all American historians he is the
most deeply and peculiarly American, yet he is
at the same time the broadest and most cosmo-

politan. The book which depicts at once the social life of the Stone Age, and the victory of the English political ideal over the ideal which France inherited from imperial Rome, is a book for all mankind and for all time. The more adequately men's historic perspective gets adjusted, the greater will it seem. Strong in its individuality, and like to nothing else, it clearly belongs, I think, among the world's few masterpieces of the highest rank, along with the works of Herodotus, Thucydides, and Gibbon.

JOHN FISKE.

CAMBRIDGE, MASS.,
February 19, 1897.

PREFACE TO THE REVISED EDITION.

SINCE this book first appeared some new documentary evidence touching it has been brought to light, and, during a recent visit to Florida, I have acquired a more exact knowledge of the localities connected with the French occupation of that region. This added information is incorporated in the present edition, which has also received some literary revision.

BOSTON, September 16, 1885.

CONTENTS.

HUGUENOTS IN FLORIDA.

CHAPTER I.

1512–1561.

EARLY SPANISH ADVENTURE.

CHAPTER II.

1550–1558.

VILLEGAGNON.

XC CONTENTS.

CONTENTS. xci

CHAPTER IX.

1565–1567.

CHARLES IX. AND PHILIP II.

CHAPTER X.

1567–1583.

DOMINIQUE DE GOURGUES.

Illustrations

VOLUME I.

INTRODUCTION.

THE springs of American civilization, unlike those of the elder world, lie revealed in the clear light of History. In appearance they are feeble; in reality, copious and full of force. Acting at the sources of life, instruments otherwise weak become mighty for good and evil, and men, lost elsewhere in the crowd, stand forth as agents of Destiny. In their toils, their sufferings, their conflicts, momentous questions were at stake, and issues vital to the future world, — the prevalence of races, the triumph of principles, health or disease, a blessing or a curse. On the obscure strife where men died by tens or by scores hung questions of as deep import for posterity as on those mighty contests of national adolescence where carnage is reckoned by thousands.

The subject to which the proposed series will be devoted is that of " France in the New World," — the attempt of Feudalism, Monarchy, and Rome to master a continent where, at this hour, half a million of bayonets are vindicating the ascendency of a regulated freedom; — Feudalism still strong in life, though enveloped and overborne by new-born Centralization; Monarchy in the flush of triumphant power; Rome, nerved by disaster, springing with renewed vitality from ashes and corruption, and ranging the earth to reconquer abroad what she had lost at home. These banded powers, pushing into the wilderness their indomitable soldiers and devoted priests, unveiled the secrets of the barbarous continent, pierced the forests, traced and mapped out the streams, planted their emblems, built their forts, and claimed all as their own. New France was all head. Under king, noble, and Jesuit, the lank, lean body would not thrive. Even commerce wore the sword, decked itself with badges of nobility, aspired to forest seigniories and hordes of savage retainers.

Along the borders of the sea an adverse power was strengthening and widening, with slow but steadfast growth, full of blood and muscle, — a body without a head. Each had its strength, each its weakness, each its own modes of vigorous life: but the one was fruitful, the other barren; the one instinct with hope, the other darkening with shadows of despair.

By name, local position, and character, one of these communities of freemen stands forth as the most conspicuous representative of this antagonism, — Liberty and Absolutism, New England and New France. The one was the offspring of a triumphant government; the other, of an oppressed and fugitive people: the one, an unflinching champion of the Roman Catholic reaction: the other, a vanguard of the Reform. Each followed its natural laws of growth, and each came to its natural result. Vitalized by the principles of its foundation, the Puritan commonwealth grew apace. New England was pre-eminently the land of material progress. Here the prize was within every man's reach; patient industry need never doubt its reward; nay, in defiance of the four Gospels, assiduity in pursuit of gain was promoted to the rank of a duty, and thrift and godliness were linked in equivocal wedlock. Politically she was free; socially she suffered from that subtle and searching oppression which the dominant opinion of a free community may exercise over the members who compose it. As a whole, she grew upon the gaze of the world, a signal example of expansive energy; but she has not been fruitful in those salient and striking forms of character which often give a dramatic life to the annals of nations far less prosperous.

We turn to New France, and all is reversed. Here was a bold attempt to crush under the exactions of a grasping hierarchy, to stifle under the curbs and trappings of a feudal monarchy, a people compassed by influences of the wildest freedom, — whose schools were the forest and the sea, whose trade was an armed barter with savages, and whose daily life a lesson of lawless independence. But this fierce spirit had its vent. The story of New France is from the first a story of war: of war — for so her founders believed — with the adversary of mankind himself; war with savage tribes and potent forest commonwealths; war with the encroaching powers of Heresy and of England. Her brave, unthinking people were stamped with the soldier's virtues and the soldier's faults; and in their leaders were displayed, on a grand and novel stage, the energies, aspirations, and passions which belong to hopes vast and vague, ill-restricted powers, and stations of command.

The growth of New England was a result of the aggregate efforts of a busy multitude, each in his narrow circle toiling for himself, to gather competence or wealth. The expansion of New France was the achievement of a gigantic ambition striving to grasp a continent. It was a vain attempt. Long and valiantly her chiefs upheld their cause, leading to battle a vassal population, warlike as themselves. Borne down by numbers from without, wasted by corruption from within, New France fell at last; and out of her fall grew revolutions whose influence to this hour is felt through every nation of the civilized world.

The French dominion is a memory of the past; and when we evoke its departed shades, they rise upon us from their graves in strange, romantic guise. Again their ghostly camp-fires seem to burn, and the fitful light is cast around on lord and vassal and black-robed priest, mingled with wild forms of savage warriors, knit in close fellowship on the same stern errand. A boundless vision grows upon us; an untamed continent; vast wastes of forest verdure; mountains silent in primeval sleep; river, lake, and glimmering pool; wilderness oceans mingling with the sky. Such was the domain which France conquered for Civilization. Plumed helmets gleamed in the shade of its forests, priestly vestments in its dens and fastnesses of ancient barbarism. Men steeped in antique learning, pale with the close breath of the cloister, here spent the noon and evening of their lives, ruled savage hordes with a mild, parental sway, and stood serene before the direst shapes of death. Men of courtly nurture, heirs to the polish of a far-reaching ancestry, here, with their dauntless hardihood, put to shame the boldest sons of toil.

This memorable but half-forgotten chapter in the book of human life can be rightly read only by lights numerous and widely scattered. The earlier period of New France was prolific in a class of publications which are often of much historic value, but of which many are exceedingly rare. The writer, however, has at length gained access to them all. Of the unpublished records of the colonies, the archives of France are of course the grand deposit; but many documents of important bearing on the subject are to be found scattered in public and private libraries, chiefly in France and Canada. The task of collection has proved abundantly irksome and laborious. It has, however, been greatly lightened by the action of the governments of New York, Massachusetts, and Canada, in collecting from Europe copies of documents having more or less relation to their own history. It has been greatly lightened, too, by a most kind co-operation, for which the writer owes obligations too many for recognition at present, but of which he trusts to make fitting acknowledgment hereafter. Yet he cannot forbear to mention the name of Mr. John Gilmary Shea of New York, to whose labors this department of American history has been so deeply indebted, and that of the Hon. Henry Black of Quebec. Nor can he refrain from

expressing his obligation to the skilful and friendly
criticism of Mr. Charles Folsom.

In this, and still more must it be the case in succeeding volumes, the amount of reading applied to
their composition is far greater than the citations
represent, much of it being of a collateral and illus-
trative nature. This was essential to a plan whose
aim it was, while scrupulously and rigorously adher-
ing to the truth of facts, to animate them with the
life of the past, and, so far as might be, clothe the
skeleton with flesh. If, at times, it may seem that
range has been allowed to fancy, it is so in appearance only ; since the minutest details of narrative or
description rest on authentic documents or on personal observation.

Faithfulness to the truth of history involves far
more than a research, however patient and scrupulous, into special facts. Such facts may be detailed with the most minute exactness, and yet
the narrative, taken as a whole, may be unmeaning
or untrue. The narrator must seek to imbue himself with the life and spirit of the time. He must
study events in their bearings near and remote ; in
the character, habits, and manners of those who took
part in them. He must himself be, as it were, a
sharer or a spectator of the action he describes.

With respect to that special research which, if in-
adequate, is still in the most emphatic sense indis-
pensable, it has been the writer's aim to exhaust the
existing material of every subject treated. While it
would be folly to claim success in such an attempt,
he has reason to hope that, so far at least as relates

to the present volume, nothing of much importance
has escaped him. With respect to the general preparation just alluded to, he has long been too fond of
his theme to neglect any means within his reach of
making his conception of it distinct and true.

To those who have aided him with information and
documents, the extreme slowness in the progress of
the work will naturally have caused surprise. This
slowness was unavoidable. During the past eighteen
years, the state of his health has exacted throughout
an extreme caution in regard to mental application,
reducing it at best within narrow and precarious
limits, and often precluding it. Indeed, for two
periods, each of several years, any attempt at bookish
occupation would have been merely suicidal. A
condition of sight arising from kindred sources has
also retarded the work, since it has never permitted
reading or writing continuously for much more than
five minutes, and often has not permitted them at all.
A previous work, " The Conspiracy of Pontiac," was
written in similar circumstances.

The writer means, if possible, to carry the present
design to its completion. Such a completion, however, will by no means be essential as regards the
individual volumes of the series, since each will form
a separate and independent work. The present
work, it will be seen, contains two distinct and completed narratives. Some progress has been made in
others.

BOSTON, January 1, 1865.

PIONEERS OF FRANCE IN THE NEW WORLD.

Part I.

HUGUENOTS IN FLORIDA.

PREFATORY NOTE

HUGUENOTS IN FLORIDA.

THE story of New France opens with a tragedy. The political and religious enmities which were soon to bathe Europe in blood broke out with an intense and concentred fury in the distant wilds of Florida. It was under equivocal auspices that Coligny and his partisans essayed to build up a Calvinist France in America, and the attempt was met by all the forces of national rivalry, personal interest, and religious hate.

This striking passage of our early history is remarkable for the fulness and precision of the authorities that illustrate it. The incidents of the Huguenot occupation of Florida are recorded by eight eye-witnesses. Their evidence is marked by an unusual accord in respect to essential facts, as well as by a minuteness of statement which vividly pictures the events described. The following are the principal authorities consulted for the main body of the narrative : —

Ribauld, *The Whole and True Discoverie of Terra Florida.* This is Captain Jean Ribaut's account of his voyage to Florida in 1562. It was " prynted at London," " newly set forthe in Englishe," in 1563, and reprinted by Hakluyt in 1582 in his black-letter tract entitled *Divers Voyages*. It is not known to exist in the original French.

L'Histoire Notable de la Floride, mise en lumière par M. Basanier (Paris, 1586). The most valuable portion of this work consists of the letters of René de Laudonnière, the French commandant in Florida in 1564–65. They are interesting, and, with necessary allowance for the position and prejudices of the writer, trustworthy.

Challeux, *Discours de l'Histoire de la Floride* (Dieppe, 1566). Challeux was a carpenter, who went to Florida in 1565. He was above sixty years of age, a zealous Huguenot, and a philosopher in his way. His story is affecting from its simplicity. Various editions of it appeared under various titles.

Le Moyne, *Brevis Narratio eorum quæ in Florida Americæ Provincia Gallis acciderunt*. Le Moyne was Laudonnière's artist. His narrative forms the Second Part of the *Grands Voyages* of De Bry (Frankfort, 1591). It is illustrated by numerous drawings made by the writer from memory, and accompanied with descriptive letter-press.

Coppie d'une Lettre venant de la Floride (Paris, 1565). This is a letter from one of the adventurers under Laudonnière. It is reprinted in the *Recueil de Pièces sur la Floride* of Ternaux-Compans. Ternaux also prints in the same volume a narrative called *Histoire mémorable du dernier Voyage faict par le Capitaine Jean Ribaut*. It is of no ɔriginal value, being compiled from Laudonnière and Challeux.

Une Requéte au Roy, faite en forme de Complainte (1566). This is a petition for redress to Charles the Ninth from the relatives of the French massacred in Florida by the Spaniards. It recounts many incidents of that tragedy.

La Reprinse de la Floride par le Cappitaine Gourgue. This is a manuscript in the Bibliothèque Nationale, printed in the *Recueil* of Ternaux-Compans. It contains a detailed account of the remarkable expedition of Dominique de Gourgues against the Spaniards in Florida in 1567–68.

Charlevoix, in his *Histoire de la Nouvelle France*, speaks of another narrative of this expedition in manuscript, preserved in the Gourgues family. A copy of it, made in 1831 by the Vicomte de Gourgues, has been placed at the writer's disposal.

Popelinière, De Thou, Wytfleit, D'Aubigné, De Laet, Brantôme, Lescarbot, Champlain, and other writers of the sixteenth and seventeenth centuries, have told or touched upon the story of the Huguenots in Florida; but they all draw their information from one or more of the sources named above.

Lettres et Papiers d'Estat du Sieur de Forquevaulx (Bibliothèque Nationale). These include the correspondence of the French and Spanish courts concerning the massacre of the Huguenots. They are printed by Gaffarel in his *Histoire de la Floride Française.*

The Spanish authorities are the following : —

Barcia (Cardenas y Cano), *Ensayo Cronologico*

para la Historia General de la Florida (Madrid,
1723). This annalist had access to original documents of great interest. Some of them are used
as material for his narrative, others are copied entire.
Of these, the most remarkable is that of Solís de las
Meras, *Memorial de todas las Jornadas de la Conquista
de la Florida.*

Francisco Lopez de Mendoza Grajales, *Relacion
de la Jornada de Pedro Menendez de Aviles en la
Florida* (*Documentos Inéditos del Archivo de Indias,*
III. 441). A French translation of this journal will
be found in the *Recueil de Pièces sur la Floride* of
Ternaux-Compans. Mendoza was chaplain of the
expedition commanded by Menendez de Avilés, and,
like Solís, he was an eye-witness of the events which
he relates.

Pedro Menendez de Avilés, *Siete Cartas escritas
al Rey, Años de* 1565 *y* 1566, MSS. These are
the despatches of the Adelantado Menendez to
Philip the Second. They were procured for the
writer, together with other documents, from the
archives of Seville, and their contents are now for the
first time made public. They consist of seventy-two
closely written foolscap pages, and are of the highest
interest and value as regards the present subject,
confirming and amplifying the statements of Solís
and Mendoza, and giving new and curious information with respect to the designs of Spain upon the
continent of North America.

It is unnecessary to specify the authorities for
the introductory and subordinate portions of the
narrative.

The writer is indebted to Mr. Buckingham Smith, for procuring copies of documents from the archives of Spain; to Mr. Bancroft, the historian of the United States, for the use of the Vicomte de Gourgues's copy of the journal describing the expedition of his ancestor against the Spaniards; and to Mr. Charles Russell Lowell, of the Boston Athenæum, and Mr. John Langdon Sibley, Librarian of Harvard College, for obliging aid in consulting books and papers.

The portrait of Menendez in this volume is a facsimile from an old Spanish engraving, of undoubted authenticity. This also was obtained through the kindness of Mr. Buckingham Smith.

PIONEERS OF FRANCE IN THE NEW WORLD.

Part I.

HUGUENOTS IN FLORIDA.

CHAPTER I.

1512–1561.

EARLY SPANISH ADVENTURE.

Spanish Voyagers. — Romance and Avarice. — Ponce de Leon. — The Fountain of Youth and the River Jordan. — Florida discovered. — Pamphilo de Narvaez. — Hernando de Soto. — His Career. — His Death. — Succeeding Voyagers. — Spanish Claim to Florida. — Spanish Jealousy of France.

Towards the close of the fifteenth century, Spain achieved her final triumph over the infidels of Granada, and made her name glorious through all generations by the discovery of America. The religious zeal and romantic daring which a long course of Moorish wars had called forth were now exalted to redoubled fervor. Every ship from the New World came freighted with marvels which put the fictions of chivalry to shame; and to the Spaniard of that day America was a region of wonder and mystery, of vague and magnificent promise. Thither adventurers hastened, thirsting for glory and for gold, and often mingling the enthusiasm of the crusader and the valor of the knight-errant with the bigotry of inquisitors and the rapacity of pirates.   They roamed over land and sea ; they climbed unknown mountains, surveyed unknown oceans, pierced the sultry intricacies of tropical forests ; while from year to year and from day to day new wonders were unfolded, new islands and archipelagoes, new regions of gold and pearl, and barbaric empires of more than Oriental wealth.   The extravagance of hope and the fever of adventure knew no bounds.   Nor is it surprising that amid such waking marvels the imagination should run wild in romantic dreams ; that between the possible and the impossible the line of distinction should be but faintly drawn, and that men should be found ready to stake life and honor in pursuit of the most insane fantasies.

Such a man was the veteran cavalier Juan Ponce de Leon.   Greedy of honors and of riches, he embarked at Porto Rico with three brigantines, bent on schemes of discovery.   But that which gave the chief stimulus to his enterprise was a story, current among the Indians of Cuba and Hispaniola, that on the island of Bimini, said to be one of the Bahamas, there was a fountain of such virtue, that, bathing in its waters, old men resumed their youth.[1]   It was said,

[1] Herrera, *Hist. General*, Dec. I. Lib. IX. c. 11 ; De Laet, *Novus Orbis*, Lib. I. c. 16 ; Garcilaso, *Hist. de la Florida*, Part I. Lib. I. c. 3 ; Gomara, *Hist. Gén. des Indes Occidentales*, Lib. II. c. 10.   Compare Peter Martyr, *De Rebus Oceanicis*, Dec. VII. c. 7, who says that the fountain was in Florida.

The story has an explanation sufficiently characteristic, having been

moreover, that on a neighboring shore might be found a river gifted with the same beneficent property, and believed by some to be no other than the Jordan.[1] Ponce de Leon found the island of Bimini, but not the fountain. Farther westward, in the latitude of thirty degrees and eight minutes, he approached an unknown land, which he named Florida, and, steering southward, explored its coast as far as the extreme point of the peninsula, when, after some farther explorations, he retraced his course to Porto Rico.

Ponce de Leon had not regained his youth, but his active spirit was unsubdued. Nine years later he attempted to plant a colony in Florida; the Indians attacked him fiercely; he was mortally wounded, and died soon afterwards in Cuba.[2]

The voyages of Garay and Vasquez de Ayllon threw new light on the discoveries of Ponce, and the general outline of the coasts of Florida became known to the Spaniards.[3] Meanwhile, Cortés had conquered Mexico, and the fame of that iniquitous but magnifi-

suggested, it is said, by the beauty of the native women, which none could resist, and which kindled the fires of youth in the veins of age.

The terms of Ponce de Leon's bargain with the King are set forth in the MS. *Capitulacion con Juan Ponce sobre Biminy.* He was to have exclusive right to the island, settle it at his own cost, and be called Adelantado of Bimini; but the King was to build and hold forts there, send agents to divide the Indians among the settlers, and receive first a tenth, afterwards a fifth, of the gold.

[1] Fontanedo in Ternaux-Compans, *Recueil sur la Floride*, 18, 19, 42. Compare Herrera, Dec. I. Lib. IX. c. 12. In allusion to this belief, the name Jordan was given eight years afterwards by Ayllon to a river of South Carolina.

[2] Hakluyt, *Voyages*, V. 333; Barcia, *Ensayo Cronologico*, 5.

[3] Peter Martyr in Hakluyt, V. 333; De Laet, Lib. IV. c. 2.

cent exploit rang through all Spain.   Many an impatient cavalier burned to achieve a kindred fortune.
To the excited fancy of the Spaniards the unknown
land of Florida seemed the seat of surpassing wealth,
and Pamphilo de Narvaez essayed to possess himself
of its fancied treasures.   Landing on its shores, and
proclaiming destruction to the Indians unless they
acknowledged the sovereignty of the Pope and the
Emperor,[1] he advanced into the forests with three
hundred men.   Nothing could exceed their sufferings.   Nowhere could they find the gold they came
to seek.   The village of Appalache, where they hoped
to gain a rich booty, offered nothing but a few mean
wigwams.   The horses gave out, and the famished
soldiers fed upon their flesh.   The men sickened,
and the Indians unceasingly harassed their march.
At length, after two hundred and eighty leagues[2] of
wandering, they found themselves on the northern
shore of the Gulf of Mexico, and desperately put to
sea in such crazy boats as their skill and means could
construct.   Cold, disease, famine, thirst, and the
fury of the waves, melted them away.   Narvaez himself perished, and of his wretched followers no more
than four escaped, reaching by land, after years of
vicissitude, the Christian settlements of New Spain.[3]

[1] *Sommation aux Habitants de la Floride,* in Ternaux-Compans, 1.

[2] Their own exaggerated reckoning.   The journey was probably
from Tampa Bay to the Appalachicola, by a circuitous route.

[3] Narrative of Alvar Nuñez Cabeça de Vaca, second in command to
Narvaez, translated by Buckingham Smith.   Cabeça de Vaca was one
of the four who escaped, and, after living for years among the tribes

The interior of the vast country then comprehended under the name of Florida still remained unexplored. The Spanish voyager, as his caravel ploughed the adjacent seas, might give full scope to his imagination, and dream that beyond the long, low margin of forest which bounded his horizon lay hid a rich harvest for some future conqueror; perhaps a second Mexico with its royal palace and sacred pyramids, or another Cuzco with its temple of the Sun, encircled with a frieze of gold.   Haunted by such visions, the ocean chivalry of Spain could not long stand idle.

Hernando de Soto was the companion of Pizarro in the conquest of Peru.   He had come to America a needy adventurer, with no other fortune than his sword and target.   But his exploits had given him fame and fortune, and he appeared at court with the retinue of a nobleman.[1]   Still, his active energies could not endure repose, and his avarice and ambition goaded him to fresh enterprises.   He asked and obtained permission to conquer Florida.   While this design was in agitation, Cabeça de Vaca, one of those who had survived the expedition of Narvaez, appeared

of Mississippi, crossed the river Mississippi near Memphis, journeyed westward by the waters of the Arkansas and Red River to New Mexico and Chihuahua, thence to Cinaloa on the Gulf of California, and thence to Mexico. The narrative is one of the most remarkable of the early relations. See also Ramusio, III. 310, and Purchas, IV. 1499, where a portion of Cabeça de Vaca is given. Also, Garcilaso, Part I. Lib. I. c. 3 ; Gomara, Lib. II. c. 11 ; De Laet, Lib. IV. c. 3 ; Barcia, *Ensayo Cronologico*, 19.

[1] *Relation of the Portuguese Gentleman of Elvas*, c. 1.   See *Descobrimiento da Florida*, c. 1, and Hakluyt, V. 483.

ın Spain, and for purposes of his own spread abroad
the mischievous falsehood, that Florida was the
richest country yet discovered.[1] De Soto's plans
were embraced with enthusiasm.   Nobles and gentlemen contended for the privilege of joining his
standard; and, setting sail with an ample armament,
he landed at the bay of Espiritu Santo, now Tampa
Bay, in Florida, with six hundred and twenty chosen
men,[2] a band as gallant and well appointed, as eager
in purpose and audacious in hope, as ever trod the
shores of the New World.   The clangor of trumpets,
the neighing of horses, the fluttering of pennons, the
glittering of helmet and lance, startled the ancient
forest with unwonted greeting.   Amid this pomp of
chivalry, religion was not forgotten.   The sacred
vessels and vestments with bread and wine for the
Eucharist were carefully provided; and De Soto
himself declared that the enterprise was undertaken
for God alone, and seemed to be the object of His
especial care.[3]   These devout marauders could not
neglect the spiritual welfare of the Indians whom
they had come to plunder; and besides fetters to
bind, and bloodhounds to hunt them, they brought
priests and monks for the saving of their souls.

---

[1] *Relation of the Gentleman of Elvas,* c. 2.

[2] *Relation of Biedma,* in Ternaux-Compans, 51.   The Gentleman of
Elvas says in round numbers six hundred.   Garcilaso de la Vega, who
is unworthy of credit, makes the number much greater.

[3] Letter from De Soto to the Municipality of Santiago, dated at
the harbor of Espiritu Santo, 9 July, 1539.   See Ternaux-Compans,
Florida, 43.

The adventurers began their march. Their story
has been often told. For month after month and
year after year, the procession of priests and cavaliers,
crossbowmen, arquebusiers, and Indian captives laden
with the baggage, still wandered on through wild
and boundless wastes, lured hither and thither by the
ignis fatuus of their hopes. They traversed great
portions of Georgia, Alabama, and Mississippi, everywhere inflicting and enduring misery, but never
approaching their phantom El Dorado. At length,
in the third year of their journeying, they reached
the banks of the Mississippi, a hundred and thirty-
two years before its second discovery by Marquette.
One of their number describes the great river as
almost half a league wide, deep, rapid, and constantly
rolling down trees and drift-wood on its turbid
current.[1]

The Spaniards crossed over at a point above the
mouth of the Arkansas. They advanced westward,
but found no treasures, — nothing indeed but hardships, and an Indian enemy, furious, writes one of
their officers, "as mad dogs."[2] They heard of a
country towards the north where maize could not be
cultivated because the vast herds of wild cattle
devoured it.[3] They penetrated so far that they
entered the range of the roving prairie tribes; for,

---

[1] *Portuguese Relation*, c. 22.   [2] Biedma, 95.

[3] *Portuguese Relation*, c. 24. A still earlier mention of the bison
occurs in the journal of Cabeça de Vaca. Thevet, in his *Singularités*,
1558, gives a picture intended to represent a bison-bull. Coronado
saw this animal in 1540, but was not, as some assert, its first discoverer

one day, as they pushed their way with difficulty across great plains covered with tall, rank grass, they met a band of savages who dwelt in lodges of skins sewed together, subsisting on game alone, and wandering perpetually from place to place.[1] Finding neither gold nor the South Sea, for both of which they had hoped, they returned to the banks of the Mississippi.

De Soto, says one of those who accompanied him, was a "stern man, and of few words." Even in the midst of reverses, his will had been law to his followers, and he had sustained himself through the depths of disappointment with the energy of a stubborn pride. But his hour was come. He fell into deep dejection, followed by an attack of fever, and soon after died miserably. To preserve his body from the Indians, his followers sank it at midnight in the river, and the sullen waters of the Mississippi buried his ambition and his hopes.[2]

The adventurers were now, with few exceptions, disgusted with the enterprise, and longed only to escape from the scene of their miseries. After a vain attempt to reach Mexico by land, they again turned back to the Mississippi, and labored, with all the resources which their desperate necessity could suggest, to construct vessels in which they might make their way to some Christian settlement. Their condition was most forlorn. Few of their horses remained alive; their baggage had been destroyed at the burn-

[1] Biedma, 91.   [2] *Portuguese Relation*, c. 30.

ing of the Indian town of Mavila, and many of the soldiers were without armor and without weapons. In place of the gallant array which, more than three years before, had left the harbor of Espiritu Santo, a company of sickly and starving men were laboring among the swampy forests of the Mississippi, some clad in skins, and some in mats woven from a kind of wild vine.[1]

Seven brigantines were finished and launched; and, trusting their lives on board these frail vessels, they descended the Mississippi, running the gantlet between hostile tribes, who fiercely attacked them. Reaching the Gulf, though not without the loss of eleven of their number, they made sail for the Spanish settlement on the river Panuco, where they arrived safely, and where the inhabitants met them with a cordial welcome. Three hundred and eleven men thus escaped with life, leaving behind them the bones of their comrades strewn broadcast through the wilderness.[2]

De Soto's fate proved an insufficient warning, for those were still found who begged a fresh commission for the conquest of Florida; but the Emperor would not hear them. A more pacific enterprise was undertaken by Cancello, a Dominican monk, who with several brother ecclesiastics undertook to convert the

---

[1] *Portuguese Relation*, c. 20. See Hakluyt, V. 515.

[2] I have followed the accounts of Biedma and the Portuguese of Elvas, rejecting the romantic narrative of Garcilaso, in which fiction is hopelessly mingled with truth.

natives to the true faith, but was murdered in the attempt.[1] Nine years later, a plan was formed for the colonization of Florida, and Guido de las Bazares sailed to explore the coasts, and find a spot suitable for the establishment.[2] After his return, a squadron, commanded by Angel de Villafañe, and freighted with supplies and men, put to sea from San Juan d'Ulloa; but the elements were adverse, and the result was a total failure.[3] Not a Spaniard had yet gained foothold in Florida.

[1] *Relation of Beteta,* Ternaux-Compans, 107; *Documentos Inéditos,* XXVI. 340. Comp. Garcilaso, Part I. Lib. I. c. 3.

[2] The spirit of this and other Spanish enterprises may be gathered from the following passage in an address to the King, signed by Dr. Pedro de Santander, and dated 15 July, 1557: —

"It is lawful that your Majesty, like a good shepherd, appointed by the hand of the Eternal Father, should tend and lead out your sheep, since the Holy Spirit has shown spreading pastures whereon are feeding lost sheep which have been snatched away by the dragon, the Demon. These pastures are the New World, wherein is comprised Florida, now in possession of the Demon, and here he makes himself adored and revered. This is the Land of Promise, possessed by idolaters, the Amorite, Amalekite, Moabite, Canaanite. This is the land promised by the Eternal Father to the faithful, since we are commanded by God in the Holy Scriptures to take it from them, being idolaters, and, by reason of their idolatry and sin, to put them all to the knife, leaving no living thing save maidens and children, their cities robbed and sacked, their walls and houses levelled to the earth."

The writer then goes into detail, proposing to occupy Florida at various points with from one thousand to fifteen hundred colonists, found a city to be called Philippina, also another at Tuscaloosa, to be called Cæsarea, another at Tallahassee, and another at Tampa Bay, where he thinks many slaves can be had. *Carta del Doctor Pedro de Santander.*

[3] The papers relating to these abortive expeditions are preserved by Ternaux-Compans.

That name, as the Spaniards of that day understood it, comprehended the whole country extending from the Atlantic on the east to the longitude of **New Mexico** on the west, and from the Gulf of **Mexico** and the River of Palms indefinitely northward towards the polar sea.[1] This vast territory was claimed by Spain in right of the discoveries of Columbus, the grant of the Pope, and the various expeditions mentioned above. England claimed it in right of the discoveries of Cabot; while France could advance **no** better title than might be derived from the voyage of Verazzano and vague traditions of earlier visits of Breton adventurers.

With restless jealousy Spain watched the domain which she could not occupy, and on France especially she kept an eye of deep distrust. When, in 1541, Cartier and Roberval essayed to plant a colony in the part of ancient Spanish Florida now called Canada, she sent spies and fitted out caravels to watch that abortive enterprise.[2] Her fears proved just. Canada, indeed, was long to remain a solitude; but, despite the Papal bounty gifting Spain with exclusive ownership of a hemisphere, France and Heresy at length took root in the sultry forests of modern Florida.

[1] Garcilaso, Part I. Lib. I. c. 2; Herrera in Purchas, III. 868; De Laet, Lib. IV. c. 13. Barcia, *Ensayo Cronologico*, An. MDCXI., speaks of Quebec as a part of Florida. In a map of the time of Henry II. of France, all North America is named Terra Florida.

[2] See various papers on this subject in the *Coleccion de Varios Documentos* of Buckingham Smith.

CHAPTER II.

1550–1558.

VILLEGAGNON.

In the middle of the sixteenth century, Spain was the incubus of Europe. Gloomy and portentous, she chilled the world with her baneful shadow. Her old feudal liberties were gone, absorbed in the despotism of Madrid. A tyranny of monks and inquisitors, with their swarms of spies and informers, their racks, their dungeons, and their fagots, crushed all freedom of thought or speech; and, while the Dominican held his reign of terror and force, the deeper Jesuit guided the mind from infancy into those narrow depths of bigotry from which it was never to escape. Commercial despotism was joined to political and religious despotism. The hands of the government were on every branch of industry. Perverse regulations, uncertain and ruinous taxes, monopolies, encouragements, prohibitions, restrictions, cramped the national energy. Mistress of the Indies, Spain swarmed with beggars. Yet, verging to decay, she had an ominous and appalling strength. Her condition was that of an athletic man penetrated with disease, which had not yet unstrung the thews and sinews formed in his days of vigor. Philip the Second could command the service of warriors and statesmen developed in the years that were past. The gathered energies of ruined feudalism were wielded by a single hand. The mysterious King, in his den in the Escorial, dreary and silent, and bent like a scribe over his papers, was the type and the champion of arbitrary power. More than the Pope himself, he was the head of Catholicity. In doctrine and in deed, the inexorable bigotry of Madrid was ever in advance of Rome.

Not so with France. She was full of life, — a discordant and struggling vitality. Her monks and priests, unlike those of Spain, were rarely either fanatics or bigots; yet not the less did they ply the rack and the fagot, and howl for heretic blood. Their all was at stake: their vast power, their bloated wealth, were wrapped up in the ancient faith. Men were burned, and women buried alive. All was in vain. To the utmost bounds of France, the leaven of the Reform was working. The Huguenots, fugitives from torture and death, found an asylum at Geneva, their city of refuge, gathering around Calvin, their great high-priest. Thence intrepid colporteurs, their lives in their hands, bore the Bible and the psalm-book to city, hamlet, and castle, to feed the rising flame. The scattered churches, pressed by a

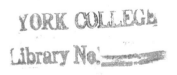

common danger, began to organize. An ecclesiastical
republic spread its ramifications through France, and
grew underground to a vigorous life, — pacific at the
outset, for the great body of its members were the
quiet *bourgeoisie*, by habit, as by faith, averse to
violence. Yet a potent fraction of the warlike *noblesse*
were also of the new faith; and above them all, pre-
eminent in character as in station, stood Gaspar de
Coligny, Admiral of France.

The old palace of the Louvre, reared by the " Roi
Chevalier " on the site of those dreary feudal towers
which of old had guarded the banks of the Seine,
held within its sculptured masonry the worthless
brood of Valois. Corruption and intrigue ran riot at
the court. Factious nobles, bishops, and cardinals,
with no God but pleasure and ambition, contended
around the throne or the sick-bed of the futile King.
Catherine de Medicis, with her stately form, her
mean spirit, her bad heart, and her fathomless depths
of duplicity, strove by every subtle art to hold the
balance of power among them. The bold, pitiless,
insatiable Guise, and his brother the Cardinal of
Lorraine, the incarnation of falsehood, rested their
ambition on the Catholic party. Their army was a
legion of priests, and the black swarms of countless
monasteries, who by the distribution of alms held in
pay the rabble of cities and starving peasants on the
lands of impoverished nobles. Montmorency, Condé,
and Navarre leaned towards the Reform, — doubtful
and inconstant chiefs, whose faith weighed light

GASPAR DE COLIGNY.

against their interests.   Yet, amid vacillation, selfishness, weakness, treachery, one great man was like a tower of trust, and this was Gaspar de Coligny.

Firm in his convictions, steeled by perils and endurance, calm, sagacious, resolute, grave even to severity, a valiant and redoubted soldier, Coligny looked abroad on the gathering storm and read its danger in advance.   He saw a strange depravity of manners; bribery and violence overriding justice; discontented nobles, and peasants ground down with taxes.   In the midst of this rottenness, the Calvinistic churches, patient and stern, were fast gathering to themselves the better life of the nation.   Among and around them tossed the surges of clerical hate.   Luxurious priests and libertine monks saw their disorders rebuked by the grave virtues of the Protestant zealots.   Their broad lands, their rich endowments, their vessels of silver and of gold, their dominion over souls, — in itself a revenue, — were all imperilled by the growing heresy.   Nor was the Reform less exacting, less intolerant, or, when its hour came, less aggressive than the ancient faith.   The storm was thickening, and it must burst soon.

When the Emperor Charles the Fifth beleaguered Algiers, his camps were deluged by a blinding tempest, and at its height the infidels made a furious sally.   A hundred Knights of Malta, on foot, wearing over their armor surcoats of crimson blazoned with the white cross, bore the brunt of the assault.   Conspicuous among them was Nicolas Durand de

Villegagnon. A Moorish cavalier, rushing upon him, pierced his arm with a lance, and wheeled to repeat the blow; but the knight leaped on the infidel, stabbed him with his dagger, flung him from his horse, and mounted in his place. Again, a Moslem host landed in Malta and beset the *Cité Notable*. The garrison was weak, disheartened, and without a leader. Villegagnon with six followers, all friends of his own, passed under cover of night through the infidel leaguer, climbed the walls by ropes lowered from above, took command, repaired the shattered towers, aiding with his own hands in the work, and animated the garrison to a resistance so stubborn that the besiegers lost heart and betook themselves to their galleys. No less was he an able and accomplished mariner, prominent among that chivalry of the sea who held the perilous verge of Christendom against the Mussulman. He claimed other laurels than those of the sword. He was a scholar, a linguist, a controversialist, potent with the tongue and with the pen, commanding in presence, eloquent and persuasive in discourse. Yet this Crichton of France had proved himself an associate nowise desirable. His sleepless intellect was matched with a spirit as restless, vain, unstable, and ambitious, as it was enterprising and bold. Addicted to dissent, and enamoured of polemics, he entered those forbidden fields of inquiry and controversy to which the Reform invited him. Undaunted by his monastic vows, he battled for heresy with tongue and pen, and in the

ear of Protestants professed himself a Protestant.
As a Commander of his Order, he quarrelled with
the Grand Master, a domineering Spaniard; and, as
Vice-Admiral of Brittany, he was deep in a feud
with the Governor of Brest.[1]　Disgusted at home,
his fancy crossed the seas.　He aspired to build for
France and himself an empire amid the tropical
splendors of Brazil.　Few could match him in the
gift of persuasion; and the intrepid seamen whose
skill and valor had run the gantlet of the English
fleet, and borne Mary Stuart of Scotland in safety to
her espousals with the Dauphin,[2] might well be
intrusted with a charge of moment so far inferior.
Henry the Second was still on the throne.　The
lance of Montgomery had not yet rid France of that
infliction.　To win a share in the rich domain of the
New World, of which Portuguese and Spanish arrogance claimed the monopoly, was the end held by

[1] Villegagnon himself has left an account in Latin of the expedi-
tion against Algiers under the title, *Caroli V. Imperatoris Expeditio in
Africam* (Paris, 1542).　Also, an account of the war at Malta, *De Bello
Melitensi* (Paris, 1553).

He is the subject of a long and erudite treatise in Bayle, *Diction-
naire Historique.*　Notices of him are also to be found in Guérin, *Navigateurs Français*, 162; Ib., *Marins Illustres*, 231 ; Lescarbot, *Hist. de la
Nouv. France* (1612), 146–217 ; La Popelinière, *Les Trois Mondes*,
III. 2.

There are extant against him a number of Calvinistic satires, in
prose and verse, — *L'Etrille de Nicolas Durand*, — *La Suffisance de
Villegaignon*, — *L'Espousette des Armoiries de Villegaignon*, etc.

[2] This was in 1548.　The English were on the watch, but Villegagnon, by a union of daring and skill, escaped them, and landed the
future Queen of Scots, then six years old, in Brittany, whence she
was carried to Paris, and affianced to the future Francis the Second.

Villegagnon before the eyes of the King. Of the Huguenots, he said not a word. For Coligny he had another language. He spoke of an asylum for persecuted religion, a Geneva in the wilderness, far from priests and monks and Francis of Guise. The Admiral gave him a ready ear; if, indeed, he himself had not first conceived the plan. Yet to the King, an active burner of Huguenots, Coligny too urged it as an enterprise, not for the Faith, but for France. In secret, Geneva was made privy to it, and Calvin himself embraced it with zeal. The enterprise, in fact, had a double character, political as well as religious. It was the reply of France, the most emphatic she had yet made, to the Papal bull which gave all the western hemisphere to Portugal and Spain; and, as if to point her answer, she sent, not Frenchmen only, but Protestant Frenchmen, to plant the fleur-de-lis on the shores of the New World.

Two vessels were made ready, in the name of the King. The body of the emigration was Huguenot, mingled with young nobles, restless, idle, and poor, with reckless artisans, and piratical sailors from the Norman and Breton seaports. They put to sea from Havre on the twelfth of July, 1555, and early in November saw the shores of Brazil. Entering the harbor of Rio Janeiro, then called Ganabara, Villegagnon landed men and stores on an island, built huts, and threw up earthworks. In anticipation of future triumphs, the whole continent, by a strange perversion of language, was called Antarctic France, while the fort received the name of Coligny.

Villegagnon signalized his new-born Protestantism by an intolerable solicitude for the manners and morals of his followers. The whip and the pillory requited the least offence. The wild and discordant crew, starved and flogged for a season into submission, conspired at length to rid themselves of him; but while they debated whether to poison him, blow him up, or murder him and his officers in their sleep, three Scotch soldiers, probably Calvinists, revealed the plot, and the vigorous hand of the commandant crushed it in the bud.

But how was the colony to subsist? Their island was too small for culture, while the mainland was infested with hostile tribes, and threatened by the Portuguese, who regarded the French occupancy as a violation of their domain.

Meanwhile, in France, Huguenot influence, aided by ardent letters sent home by Villegagnon in the returning ships, was urging on the work. Nor were the Catholic chiefs averse to an enterprise which, by colonizing heresy, might tend to relieve France of its presence. Another embarkation was prepared, in the name of Henry the Second, under Bois-Lecomte, a nephew of Villegagnon. Most of the emigrants were Huguenots. Geneva sent a large deputation, and among them several ministers, full of zeal for their land of promise and their new church in the wilderness. There were five young women, also, with a matron to watch over them.   Soldiers, emigrants, and sailors, two hundred and ninety in all, were embarked in three vessels; and, to the sound of cannon, drums, fifes, and trumpets, they unfurled their sails at Honfleur.   They were no sooner on the high seas than the piratical character of the Norman sailors, in no way exceptional at that day, began to declare itself.   They hailed every vessel weaker than themselves, pretended to be short of provisions, and demanded leave to buy them; then, boarding the stranger, plundered her from stem to stern.   After a passage of four months, on the ninth of March, 1557, they entered the port of Ganabara, and saw the fleur-de-lis floating above the walls of Fort Coligny.   Amid salutes of cannon, the boats, crowded with sea-worn emigrants, moved towards the landing.   It was an edifying scene when Villegagnon, in the picturesque attire which marked the warlike nobles of the period, came down to the shore to greet the sombre ministers of Calvin.   With hands uplifted and eyes raised to heaven, he bade them welcome to the new asylum of the faithful; then launched into a long harangue full of zeal and unction.[1]   His discourse finished, he led

---

[1] De Léry, *Historia Navigationis in Brasiliam* (1586), 43.   De Léry was one of the ministers.   His account is long and very curious.   His work was published in French, in 1578 and 1611.   The Latin version has appeared under several forms, and is to be found in the Second Part of De Bry, decorated with a profusion of engravings, including portraits of a great variety of devils, with which, it seems, Brazil was overrun, conspicuous among whom is one with the body of a bear and the head of a man.   This ungainly fiend is also depicted in the edition of 1586.   The conception, a novelty in demonology, was clearly derived

the way to the dining-hall. If the redundancy of spiritual aliment had surpassed their expectations, the ministers were little prepared for the meagre provision which awaited their temporal cravings; for, with appetites whetted by the sea, they found themselves seated at a board whereof, as one of them complains, the choicest dish was a dried fish, and the only beverage rain-water. They found their consolation in the inward graces of the commandant, whom they likened to the Apostle Paul.

For a time all was ardor and hope. Men of birth and station, and the ministers themselves, labored with pick and shovel to finish the fort. Every day exhortations, sermons, prayers, followed in close succession, and Villegagnon was always present, kneeling on a velvet cushion brought after him by a page. Soon, however, he fell into sharp controversy with the ministers upon points of faith. Among the emigrants was a student of the Sorbonne, one Cointac, between whom and the ministers arose a fierce and unintermitted war of words. Is it lawful to mix water with the wine of the Eucharist? May the sacramental bread be made of meal of Indian corn? These and similar points of dispute filled the fort

from ancient representations of that singular product of Brazil, the sloth. In the curious work of André Thevet, *Les Singularités de la France Antarctique, autrement nommée Amérique*, published in 1558, appears the portraiture of this animal, the body being that "d'un petit ours," and the face that of an intelligent man. Thevet, however, though a firm believer in devils of all kinds, suspects nothing demoniacal in his sloth, which he held for some time in captivity, and describes as "une beste assez estrange."

with wranglings, begetting cliques, factions, and feuds without number. Villegagnon took part with the student, and between them they devised a new doctrine, abhorrent alike to Geneva and to Rome. The advent of this nondescript heresy was the signal of redoubled strife.[1] The dogmatic stiffness of the Geneva ministers chafed Villegagnon to fury. He felt himself, too, in a false position. On one side he depended on the Protestant, Coligny; on the other, he feared the Court. There were Catholics in the colony who might report him as an open heretic. On this point his doubts were set at rest; for a ship from France brought him a letter from the Cardinal of Lorraine, couched, it is said, in terms which restored him forthwith to the bosom of the Church. Villegagnon now affirmed that he had been deceived in Calvin, and pronounced him a "frightful heretic." He became despotic beyond measure, and would bear no opposition. The ministers, reduced nearly to starvation, found themselves under a tyranny worse than that from which they had fled.

At length he drove them from the fort, and forced them to bivouac on the mainland, at the risk of being butchered by Indians, until a vessel loading with Brazil-wood in the harbor should be ready to carry them back to France. Having rid himself of the ministers, he caused three of the more zealous

---

[1] The history of these theological squabbles is given in detail in the *Histoire des Choses Mémorables advenues en la Terre du Brésil* (Genêve, 1561). The author was an eye-witness. De Léry also enlarges upon them.

Calvinists to be seized, dragged to the edge of a rock, and thrown into the sea.[1] A fourth, equally obnoxious, but who, being a tailor, could ill be spared, was permitted to live on condition of recantation. Then, mustering the colonists, he warned them to shun the heresies of Luther and Calvin; threatened that all who openly professed those detestable doctrines should share the fate of their three comrades; and, his harangue over, feasted the whole assembly, in token, says the narrator, of joy and triumph.[2]

Meanwhile, in their crazy vessel, the banished ministers drifted slowly on their way. Storms fell upon them, their provisions failed, their water-casks were empty, and, tossing in the wilderness of waves, or rocking on the long swells of subsiding gales, they sank almost to despair. In their famine they chewed the Brazil-wood with which the vessel was laden, devoured every scrap of leather, singed and ate the horn of lanterns, hunted rats through the hold, and sold them to each other at enormous prices. At length, stretched on the deck, sick, listless, attenuated, and scarcely able to move a limb, they descried across the waste of sea the faint, cloud-like line that marked the coast of Brittany. Their perils were not past; for, if we may believe one of them, Jean de Léry, they bore a sealed letter from Villegagnon to

---

[1] *Histoire des Choses Mémorables*, 44.

[2] *Histoire des Choses Mémorables*, 46. Compare Barré, *Lettres sur la Navigation du Chevalier de Villegagnon* (Paris, 1558). Original documents concerning Villegagnon will be found in Gaffarel, *Brésil Français*, Appendix.

the magistrates of the first French port at which they might arrive. It denounced them as heretics, worthy to be burned. Happily, the magistrates leaned to the Reform, and the malice of the commandant failed of its victims.

Villegagnon himself soon sailed for France, leaving the wretched colony to its fate. He presently entered the lists against Calvin, and engaged him in a hot controversial war, in which, according to some of his contemporaries, the knight often worsted the theologian at his own weapons. Before the year 1558 was closed, Ganabara fell a prey to the Portuguese. They set upon it in force, battered down the fort, and slew the feeble garrison, or drove them to a miserable refuge among the Indians. Spain and Portugal made good their claim to the vast domain, the mighty vegetation, and undeveloped riches of "Antarctic France."

CHAPTER III.

1562, 1563.

JEAN RIBAUT.

The Huguenot Party, its motley Character. — Ribaut sails for Florida. — The River of May. — Hopes. — Illusions. — Port Royal. — Charlesfort. — Frolic. — Improvidence. — Famine. — Mutiny. — Florida abandoned. — Desperation. — Cannibalism.

In the year 1562 a cloud of black and deadly portent was thickening over France. Surely and swiftly she glided towards the abyss of the religious wars. None could pierce the future, perhaps none dared to contemplate it: the wild rage of fanaticism and hate, friend grappling with friend, brother with brother, father with son; altars profaned, hearthstones made desolate, the robes of Justice herself bedrenched with murder. In the gloom without lay Spain, imminent and terrible. As on the hill by the field of Dreux, her veteran bands of pikemen, dark masses of organized ferocity, stood biding their time while the battle surged below, and then swept downward to the slaughter, — so did Spain watch and wait to trample and crush the hope of humanity.

In these days of fear, a second Huguenot colony sailed for the New World. The calm, stern man

who represented and led the Protestantism of France
felt to his inmost heart the peril of the time. He
would fain build up a city of refuge for the persecuted sect. Yet Gaspar de Coligny, too high in
power and rank to be openly assailed, was forced to
act with caution. He must act, too, in the name of
the Crown, and in virtue of his office of Admiral
of France. A nobleman and a soldier, — for the
Admiral of France was no seaman, — he shared the
ideas and habits of his class; nor is there reason to
believe him to have been in advance of his time in a
knowledge of the principles of successful colonization. His scheme promised a military colony, not
a free commonwealth. The Huguenot party was
already a political as well as a religious party. At
its foundation lay the religious element, represented
by Geneva, the martyrs, and the devoted fugitives
who sang the psalms of Marot among rocks and
caverns. Joined to these were numbers on whom
the faith sat lightly, whose hope was in commotion
and change. Of the latter, in great part, was the
Huguenot *noblesse*, from Condé, who aspired to the
crown,

> " Ce petit homme tant joli,
>   Qui toujours chante, toujours rit,"

to the younger son of the impoverished seigneur
whose patrimony was his sword. More than this,
the restless, the factious, and the discontented, began
to link their fortunes to a party whose triumph would
involve confiscation of the wealth of the only rich

class in France.   An element of the great revolution
was already mingling in the strife of religions.

America was still a land of wonder.   The ancient
spell still hung unbroken over the wild, vast world
of mystery beyond the sea, — a land of romance,
adventure, and gold.

Fifty-eight years later the Puritans landed on the
sands of Massachusetts Bay.   The illusion was gone,
— the *ignis fatuus* of adventure, the dream of wealth.
The rugged wilderness offered only a stern and hard-
won independence.   In their own hearts, and not in
the promptings of a great leader or the patronage of
an equivocal government, their enterprise found its
birth and its achievement.   They were of the boldest
and most earnest of their sect.   There were such
among the French disciples of Calvin; but no May-
flower ever sailed from a port of France.   Coligny's
colonists were of a different stamp, and widely
different was their fate.

An excellent seaman and stanch Protestant, Jean
Ribaut of Dieppe, commanded the expedition.   Under
him, besides sailors, were a band of veteran soldiers,
and a few young nobles.   Embarked in two of those
antiquated craft whose high poops and tub-like pro-
portions are preserved in the old engravings of De
Bry, they sailed from Havre on the eighteenth of
February, 1562.[1]   They crossed the Atlantic, and on
the thirtieth of April, in the latitude of twenty-nine
and a half degrees, saw the long, low line where the

[1] Delaborde, *Gaspard de Coligny*, II. 14, 440.

wilderness of waves met the wilderness of woods. It
was the coast of Florida. They soon descried a jut-
ting point, which they called French Cape, perhaps
one of the headlands of Matanzas Inlet. They
turned their prows northward, coasting the fringes
of that waste of verdure which rolled in shadowy
undulation far to the unknown West.

On the next morning, the first of May, they found
themselves off the mouth of a great river. Riding
at anchor on a sunny sea, they lowered their boats,
crossed the bar that obstructed the entrance, and
floated on a basin of deep and sheltered water, "boyl-
ing and roaring," says Ribaut, "through the multitude of all kind of fish." Indians were running
along the beach, and out upon the sand-bars, beckon-
ing them to land. They pushed their boats ashore
and disembarked, — sailors, soldiers, and eager young
nobles. Corselet and morion, arquebuse and halberd,
flashed in the sun that flickered through innumerable
leaves, as, kneeling on the ground, they gave thanks
to God, who had guided their voyage to an issue full
of promise. The Indians, seated gravely under the
neighboring trees, looked on in silent respect, thinking that they worshipped the sun. "They be all
naked and of a goodly stature, mightie, and as well
shapen and proportioned of body as any people in yᵉ
world; and the fore part of their body and armes be
painted with pretie deuised workes, of Azure, red,
and blacke, so well and so properly as the best
Painter of Europe could not amende it." With their

RIBAUT AND HIS FOLLOWERS.

squaws and children, they presently drew near, and, strewing the earth with laurel boughs, sat down among the Frenchmen. Their visitors were much pleased with them, and Ribaut gave the chief, whom he calls the king, a robe of blue cloth, worked in yellow with the regal fleur-de-lis.

But Ribaut and his followers, just escaped from the dull prison of their ships, were intent on admiring the wild scenes around them. Never had they known a fairer May-day. The quaint old narrative is exuberant with delight. The tranquil air, the warm sun, woods fresh with young verdure, meadows bright with flowers; the palm, the cypress, the pine, the magnolia; the grazing deer; herons, curlews, bitterns, woodcock, and unknown water-fowl that waded in the ripple of the beach; cedars bearded from crown to root with long, gray moss; huge oaks smothering in the folds of enormous grape-vines; — such were the objects that greeted them in their roamings, till their new-discovered land seemed "the fairest, fruitfullest, and pleasantest of al the world."

They found a tree covered with caterpillars, and hereupon the ancient black-letter says: "Also there be Silke wormes in meruielous number, a great deale fairer and better then be our silk wormes. To bee short, it is a thing vnspeakable to consider the thinges that bee seene there, and shalbe founde more and more in this incomperable lande." [1]

---

[1] *The True and Last Discoverie of Florida, made by Captain John Ribault, in the Yeere* 1562, *dedicated to a great Nobleman in Fraunce.*

Above all, it was plain to their excited fancy that the country was rich in gold and silver, turquoises and pearls. One of these last, "as great as an Acorne at yͤ least," hung from the neck of an Indian who stood near their boats as they re-embarked. They gathered, too, from the signs of their savage visitors, that the wonderful land of Cibola, with its seven cities and its untold riches, was distant but twenty days' journey by water. In truth, it was two thousand miles westward, and its wealth a fable.

They named the river the River of May. It is now the St. John's. "And on the next morning," says Ribault, "we returned to land againe, accompanied with the Captaines, Gentlemen, and Souldiers, and others of our small troope, carrying with us a Pillour or columne of harde stone, our king's armes graved therein, to plant and set the same in the enterie of the Porte; and being come thither we espied on the south syde of the Riuer a place very fitte for that purpose upon a little hill compassed with Cypres, Bayes, Paulmes, and other trees, with sweete smelling and pleasant shrubbes." Here they set the column, and then, again embarking, held their course northward, happy in that benign decree

and translated into Englishe by one Thomas Hackit. This is Ribaut's journal, which seems not to exist in the original. The translation is contained in the rare black-letter tract of Hakluyt called *Divers Voyages* (London, 1582), a copy of which is in the library of Harvard College. It has been reprinted by the Hakluyt Society. The journal first appeared in 1563, under the title of *The Whole and True Discoverie of Terra Florida* (*Englished The Florishing Land*). This edition is of extreme rarity.

which locks from mortal eyes the secrets of the future.

Next they anchored near Fernandina, and to a neighboring river, probably the St. Mary's, gave the name of the Seine. Here, as morning broke on the fresh, moist meadows hung with mists, and on broad reaches of inland waters which seemed like lakes, they were tempted to land again, and soon "espied an innumerable number of footesteps of great Hartes and Hindes of a wonderfull greatnesse, the steppes being all fresh and new, and it seemeth that the people doe nourish them like tame Cattell." By two or three weeks of exploration they seem to have gained a clear idea of this rich semi-aquatic region. Ribaut describes it as "a countrie full of hauens, riuers, and Ilands, of such fruitfulnes as cannot with tongue be expressed." Slowly moving northward, they named each river, or inlet supposed to be a river, after some stream of France, — the Loire, the Charente, the Garonne, the Gironde. At length, opening betwixt flat and sandy shores, they saw a commodious haven, and named it Port Royal.

On the twenty-seventh of May they crossed the bar where the war-ships of Dupont crossed three hundred years later, passed Hilton Head, and held their course along the peaceful bosom of Broad River.[1] On the left they saw a stream which they

---

[1] Ribaut thinks that the Broad River of Port Royal is the Jordan of the Spanish navigator Vasquez de Ayllon, who was here in 1520, and gave the name of St. Helena to a neighboring cape (Garcilaso, *Florida del Inca*). The adjacent district, now called St. Helena, is the Chicora of the old Spanish maps.

named Libourne, probably Skull Creek; on the right,
a wide river, probably the Beaufort. When they
landed, all was solitude. The frightened Indians
had fled, but they lured them back with knives,
beads, and looking-glasses, and enticed two of them
on board their ships. Here, by feeding, clothing,
and caressing them, they tried to wean them from
their fears, thinking to carry them to France, in
obedience to a command of Catherine de Medicis;[1]
but the captive warriors moaned and lamented day
and night, and at length made their escape.

Ranging the woods, they found them full of game,
wild turkeys and partridges, bears and lynxes. Two
deer, of unusual size, leaped from the underbrush.
Cross-bow and arquebuse were brought to the level;
but the Huguenot captain, "moved with the singular
fairness and bigness of them," forbade his men to
shoot.

Preliminary exploration, not immediate settlement,
had been the object of the voyage; but all was still
rose-color in the eyes of the voyagers, and many of
their number would gladly linger in the New Canaan.
Ribaut was more than willing to humor them. He
mustered his company on deck, and made them a
harangue. He appealed to their courage and their
patriotism, told them how, from a mean origin, men
rise by enterprise and daring to fame and fortune,
and demanded who among them would stay behind
and hold Port Royal for the King. The greater part

---

[1] Laudonnière in Basanier, 14.

came forward, and "with such a good will and joly corage," writes the commander, "as we had much to do to stay their importunitie." Thirty were chosen, and Albert de Pierria was named to command them.

A fort was begun on a small stream called the Chenonceau, probably Archer's Creek, about six miles from the site of Beaufort.[1] They named it Charlesfort, in honor of the unhappy son of Catherine de Medicis, Charles the Ninth, the future hero of St. Bartholomew. Ammunition and stores were sent on shore, and on the eleventh of June, with his diminished company, Ribaut again embarked and spread his sails for France.

From the beach at Hilton Head, Albert and his companions might watch the receding ships, growing less and less on the vast expanse of blue, dwindling to faint specks, then vanishing on the pale verge of the waters. They were alone in those fearful solitudes. From the north pole to Mexico there was no Christian denizen but they.

The pressing question was how they were to subsist. Their thought was not of subsistence, but of gold. Of the thirty, the greater number were soldiers and sailors, with a few gentlemen; that is to say, men of the sword, born within the pale of nobility, who at home could neither labor nor trade without derogation from their rank. For a time they

---

[1] No trace of this fort has been found. The old fort of which the remains may be seen a little below Beaufort is of later date.

busied themselves with finishing their fort, and, this done, set forth in quest of adventures.

The Indians had lost fear of them. Ribaut had enjoined upon them to use all kindness and gentleness in their dealing with the men of the woods; and they more than obeyed him. They were soon hand and glove with chiefs, warriors, and squaws; and as with Indians the adage that familiarity breeds contempt holds with peculiar force, they quickly divested themselves of the prestige which had attached at the outset to their supposed character of children of the Sun. Good-will, however, remained, and this the colonists abused to the utmost.

Roaming by river, swamp, and forest, they visited in turn the villages of five petty chiefs, whom they called kings, feasting everywhere on hominy, beans, and game, and loaded with gifts. One of these chiefs, named Audusta, invited them to the grand religious festival of his tribe. When they arrived, they found the village alive with preparation, and troops of women busied in sweeping the great circular area where the ceremonies were to take place. But as the noisy and impertinent guests showed a disposition to undue merriment, the chief shut them all in his wigwam, lest their Gentile eyes should profane the mysteries. Here, immured in darkness, they listened to the howls, yelpings, and lugubrious songs that resounded from without. One of them, however, by some artifice, contrived to escape, hid behind a bush, and saw the whole solemnity, — the proces-

sion of the medicine-men and the bedaubed and
befeathered warriors; the drumming, dancing, and
stamping; the wild lamentation of the women as they
gashed the arms of the young girls with sharp mussel-
shells, and flung the blood into the air with dismal
outcries.   A scene of ravenous feasting followed, in
which the French, released from durance, were
summoned to share.

After the carousal they returned to Charlesfort,
where they were soon pinched with hunger.   The Indians, never niggardly of food, brought them supplies
as long as their own lasted; but the harvest was not yet
ripe, and their means did not match their good-will.
They told the French of two other kings, Ouadé and
Couexis, who dwelt towards the south, and were rich
beyond belief in maize, beans, and squashes.   The
mendicant colonists embarked without delay, and,
with an Indian guide, steered for the wigwams of
these potentates, not by the open sea, but by a per-
plexing inland navigation, including, as it seems,
Calibogue Sound and neighboring waters.   Reaching
the friendly villages, on or near the Savannah, they
were feasted to repletion, and their boat was laden
with vegetables and corn.   They returned rejoicing;
but their joy was short.   Their store-house at
Charlesfort, taking fire in the night, burned to the
ground, and with it their newly acquired stock.
Once more they set out for the realms of King Ouadé,
and once more returned laden with supplies.   Nay,
the generous savage assured them that, so long as his

cornfields yielded their harvests, his friends should
not want.

How long this friendship would have lasted may
well be doubted. With the perception that the
dependants on their bounty were no demigods, but a
crew of idle and helpless beggars, respect would soon
have changed to contempt, and contempt to ill-will.
But it was not to Indian war-clubs that the infant
colony was to owe its ruin. It carried within itself
its own destruction. The ill-assorted band of lands-
men and sailors surrounded by that influence of the
wilderness which wakens the dormant savage in the
breasts of men, soon fell into quarrels. Albert, a
rude soldier, with a thousand leagues of ocean betwixt
him and responsibility, grew harsh, domineering, and
violent beyond endurance. None could question or
oppose him without peril of death. He hanged with
his own hands a drummer who had fallen under his
displeasure, and banished a soldier, named La Chère,
to a solitary island, three leagues from the fort,
where he left him to starve. For a time his comrades chafed in smothered fury. The crisis came at
length. A few of the fiercer spirits leagued together,
assailed their tyrant, murdered him, delivered the
famished soldier, and called to the command one
Nicolas Barré, a man of merit. Barré took the command, and thenceforth there was peace.

Peace, such as it was, with famine, homesickness,
and disgust. The rough ramparts and rude buildings of Charlesfort, hatefully familiar to their weary

eyes, the sweltering forest, the glassy river, the
eternal silence of the lifeless wilds around them,
oppressed the senses and the spirits.   They dreamed
of ease, of home, of pleasures across the sea, of the
evening cup on the bench before the cabaret, and
dances with kind wenches of Dieppe.   But how to
escape?   A continent was their solitary prison, and
the pitiless Atlantic shut them in.   Not one of them
knew how to build a ship; but Ribaut had left them
a forge, with tools and iron, and strong desire supplied the place of skill.   Trees were hewn down and
the work begun.   Had they put forth to maintain
themselves at Port Royal the energy and resource
which they exerted to escape from it, they might
have laid the corner-stone of a solid colony.

All, gentle and simple, labored with equal zeal.
They calked the seams with the long moss which
hung in profusion from the neighboring trees; the
pines supplied them with pitch; the Indians made
for them a kind of cordage; and for sails they sewed
together their shirts and bedding.   At length a brigantine worthy of Robinson Crusoe floated on the
waters of the Chenonceau.   They laid in what provision they could, gave all that remained of their
goods to the Indians, embarked, descended the river,
and put to sea.   A fair wind filled their patchwork
sails and bore them from the hated coast.   Day after
day they held their course, till at length the breeze
died away and a breathless calm fell on the waters.
Florida was far behind; France farther yet before.

Floating idly on the glassy waste, the craft lay
motionless. Their supplies gave out. Twelve ker-
nels of maize a day were each man's portion; then
the maize failed, and they ate their shoes and leather
jerkins. The water-barrels were drained, and they
tried to slake their thirst with brine. Several died,
and the rest, giddy with exhaustion and crazed with
thirst, were forced to ceaseless labor, bailing out the
water that gushed through every seam. Head-winds
set in, increasing to a gale, and the wretched brigantine, with sails close-reefed, tossed among the savage
billows at the mercy of the storm. A heavy sea
rolled down upon her, and burst the bulwarks on the
windward side. The surges broke over her, and,
clinging with desperate gripe to spars and cordage,
the drenched voyagers gave up all for lost. At
length she righted. The gale subsided, the wind
changed, and the crazy, water-logged vessel again
bore slowly towards France.

Gnawed with famine, they counted the leagues of
barren ocean that still stretched before, and gazed on
each other with haggard wolfish eyes, till a whisper
passed from man to man that one, by his death,
might ransom all the rest. The lot was cast, and
it fell on La Chère, the same wretched man whom
Albert had doomed to starvation on a lonely island.
They killed him, and with ravenous avidity portioned
out his flesh. The hideous repast sustained them till
the land rose in sight, when, it is said, in a delirium
of joy, they could no longer steer their vessel, but let

her drift at the will of the tide.   A small English
bark bore down upon them, took them all on board,
and, after landing the feeblest, carried the rest
prisoners to Queen Elizabeth.[1]

Thus closed another of those scenes of woe whose
lurid clouds are thickly piled around the stormy dawn
of American history.   It was the opening act of a
wild and tragic drama.

[1] For all the latter part of the chapter, the authority is the first of
the three long letters of René de Laudonnière, companion of Ribaut
and his successor in command.   They are contained in the *Histoire
Notable de la Floride*, compiled by Basanier (Paris, 1586), and are
also to be found, quaintly " done into English," in the third volume of
Hakluyt's great collection.   In the main, they are entitled to much
confidence.

CHAPTER IV.

1564.

LAUDONNIÈRE.

On the twenty-fifth of June, 1564, a French squadron anchored a second time off the mouth of the River of May. There were three vessels, the smallest of sixty tons, the largest of one hundred and twenty, all crowded with men. René de Laudonnière held command. He was of a noble race of Poitou, attached to the house of Châtillon, of which Coligny was the head; pious, we are told, and an excellent marine officer. An engraving, purporting to be his likeness, shows us a slender figure, leaning against the mast, booted to the thigh, with slouched hat and plume, slashed doublet, and short cloak. His thin oval face, with curled moustache and close-trimmed beard, wears a somewhat pensive look, as if already shadowed by the destiny that awaited him.[1]

The intervening year since Ribaut's voyage had been a dark year for France. From the peaceful

[1] See Guérin, *Navigateurs Français*, 180. The authenticity of the portrait is doubtful.

solitude of the River of May, that voyager returned to a land reeking with slaughter. But the carnival of bigotry and hate had found a pause. The Peace of Amboise had been signed. The fierce monk choked down his venom; the soldier sheathed his sword, the assassin his dagger; rival chiefs grasped hands, and masked their rancor under hollow smiles. The king and the queen-mother, helpless amid the storm of factions which threatened their destruction, smiled now on Condé, now on Guise, — gave ear to the Cardinal of Lorraine, or listened in secret to the emissaries of Theodore Beza. Coligny was again strong at Court. He used his opportunity, and solicited with success the means of renewing his enterprise of colonization.[1]

Men were mustered for the work. In name, at least, they were all Huguenots; yet now, as before, the staple of the projected colony was unsound, — soldiers, paid out of the royal treasury, hired artisans and tradesmen, with a swarm of volunteers from the young Huguenot nobles, whose restless swords had rusted in their scabbards since the peace. The foundation-stone was forgotten. There were no tillers of the soil. Such, indeed, were rare among the Huguenots; for the dull peasants who guided the plough clung with blind tenacity to the ancient faith. Adventurous gentlemen, reckless soldiers, discontented tradesmen, all keen for novelty and heated with dreams of wealth, — these were they who would

---

[1] Delaborde, *Gaspard de Coligny*, II. 443

build for their country and their religion an empire
beyond the sea.[1]

On Thursday, the twenty-second of June, Laudonnière saw the low coast-line of Florida, and entered
the harbor of St. Augustine, which he named the
River of Dolphins, "because that at mine arrival I
saw there a great number of Dolphins which were
playing in the mouth thereof."[2]   Then he bore northward, following the coast till, on the twenty-fifth, he
reached the mouth of the St. John's or River of May.
The vessels anchored, the boats were lowered, and
he landed with his principal followers on the south
shore, near the present village of Mayport.   It was
the very spot where he had landed with Ribaut two
years before.   They were scarcely on shore when
they saw an Indian chief, "which having espied us
cryed very far off, *Antipola ! Antipola !* and being so
joyful that he could not containe himselfe, he came
to meet us accompanied with two of his sonnes, as

---

[1] The principal authorities for this part of the narrative are Laudonnière and his artist, Le Moyne. Laudonnière's letters were published
in 1586, under the title *L'Histoire Notable de la Floride, mise en lumière
par M. Basanier.* See also Hakluyt's *Voyages,* III. (1812). Le Moyne
was employed to make maps and drawings of the country. His maps
are curiously inexact. His drawings are spirited, and, with many
allowances, give useful hints concerning the habits of the natives.
They are engraved in the *Grands Voyages* of De Bry, Part II. (Frankfort, 1591). To each is appended a "declaratio," or explanatory
remarks. The same work contains the artist's personal narrative, the
Brevis Narratio. In the *Recueil de Pièces sur la Floride* of Ternaux-
Compans is a letter from one of the adventurers.

[2] Second letter of Laudonnière; contemporary translation in Hakluyt, III.

faire and mightie persons as might be found in al the
world.   There was in their trayne a great number of
men and women which stil made very much of us,
and by signes made us understand how glad they
were of our arrivall.   This good entertainment past,
the Paracoussy [chief] prayed me to goe see the pillar
which we had erected in the voyage of John Ribault.''
The Indians, regarding it with mysterious awe, had
crowned it with evergreens, and placed baskets full
of maize before it as an offering.

The chief then took Laudonnière by the hand,
telling him that he was named Satouriona, and pointed
out the extent of his dominions, far up the river and
along the adjacent coasts.   One of his sons, a man
"perfect in beautie, wisedome, and honest sobrietie,"
then gave the French commander a wedge of silver,
and received some trifles in return, after which the
voyagers went back to their ships.   "I prayse God
continually," says Laudonnière, "for the great love I
have found in these savages."

In the morning the French landed again, and
found their new friends on the same spot, to the
number of eighty or more, seated under a shelter of
boughs, in festal attire of smoke-tanned deer-skins,
painted in many colors.   The party then rowed up
the river, the Indians following them along the shore.
As they advanced, coasting the borders of a great
marsh that lay upon their left, the St. John's spread
before them in vast sheets of glistening water, almost
level with its flat, sedgy shores, the haunt of alli-

gators, and the resort of innumerable birds. Beyond the marsh, some five miles from the mouth of the river, they saw a ridge of high ground abutting on the water, which, flowing beneath in a deep, strong current, had undermined it, and left a steep front of yellowish sand. This was the hill now called St. John's Bluff. Here they landed and entered the woods, where Laudonnière stopped to rest while his lieutenant, Ottigny, with a sergeant and a few soldiers, went to explore the country.

They pushed their way through the thickets till they were stopped by a marsh choked with reeds, at the edge of which, under a great laurel-tree, they had seated themselves to rest, overcome with the summer heat, when five Indians suddenly appeared, peering timidly at them from among the bushes. Some of the men went towards them with signs of friendship, on which, taking heart, they drew near, and one of them, who was evidently a chief, made a long speech, inviting the strangers to their dwellings. The way was across the marsh, through which they carried the lieutenant and two or three of the soldiers on their backs, while the rest circled by a narrow path through the woods. When they reached the lodges, a crowd of Indians came out "to receive our men gallantly, and feast them after their manner." One of them brought a large earthen vessel full of spring water, which was served out to each in turn in a wooden cup. But what most astonished the French was a venerable chief, who assured them that he was the

father of five successive generations, and that he had
lived two hundred and fifty years. Opposite sat a
still more ancient veteran, the father of the first,
shrunken to a mere anatomy, and "seeming to be
rather a dead carkeis than a living body." "Also,"
pursues the history, "his age was so great that the
good man had lost his sight, and could not speak one
onely word but with exceeding great paine."[1] In
spite of his dismal condition, the visitors were told
that he might expect to live, in the course of nature,
thirty or forty years more. As the two patriarchs
sat face to face, half hidden with their streaming
white hair, Ottigny and his credulous soldiers looked
from one to the other, lost in speechless admiration.

One of these veterans made a parting present to
his guests of two young eagles, and Ottigny and his
followers returned to report what they had seen.
Laudonnière was waiting for them on the side of the
hill; and now, he says, "I went right to the toppe
thereof, where we found nothing else but Cedars,
Palme, and Baytrees of so sovereigne odour that
Baulme smelleth nothing like in comparison." From
this high standpoint they surveyed their Canaan. The
unruffled river lay before them, with its marshy
islands overgrown with sedge and bulrushes; while
on the farther side the flat, green meadows spread
mile on mile, veined with countless creeks and belts
of torpid water, and bounded leagues away by the

[1] Laudonnière in Hakluyt, III. 388; Basanier, fol. 40; *Coppie d'une
Lettre venant de la Floride* in Ternaux-Compans, *Floride*, 233.

verge of the dim pine forest. On the right, the sea glistened along the horizon; and on the left, the St. John's stretched westward between verdant shores, a highway to their fancied Eldorado. "Briefly," writes Laudonnière, "the place is so pleasant that those which are melancholicke would be inforced to change their humour."

On their way back to the ships they stopped for another parley with the chief Satouriona, and Laudonnière eagerly asked where he had got the wedge of silver that he gave him in the morning. The chief told him by signs, that he had taken it in war from a people called Thimagoas, who lived higher up the river, and who were his mortal enemies; on which the French captain had the folly to promise that he would join in an expedition against them. Satouriona was delighted, and declared that, if he kept his word, he should have gold and silver to his heart's content.

Man and nature alike seemed to mark the borders of the River of May as the site of the new colony; for here, around the Indian towns, the harvests of maize, beans, and pumpkins promised abundant food, while the river opened a ready way to the mines of gold and silver and the stores of barbaric wealth which glittered before the dreaming vision of the colonists. Yet, the better to satisfy himself and his men, Laudonnière weighed anchor, and sailed for a time along the neighboring coasts. Returning, confirmed in his first impression, he set out with a party of officers and soldiers to explore the borders of the chosen

stream. The day was hot. The sun beat fiercely on
the woollen caps and heavy doublets of the men, till
at length they gained the shade of one of those deep
forests of pine where the dead, hot air is thick with
resinous odors, and the earth, carpeted with fallen
leaves, gives no sound beneath the foot. Yet, in the
stillness, deer leaped up on all sides as they moved
along. Then they emerged into sunlight. A meadow
was before them, a running brook, and a wall of
encircling forests. The men called it the Vale of
Laudonnière. The afternoon was spent, and the sun
was near its setting, when they reached the bank of
the river. They strewed the ground with boughs
and leaves, and, stretched on that sylvan couch, slept
the sleep of travel-worn and weary men.

They were roused at daybreak by sound of trumpet,
and after singing a psalm they set themselves to their
task. It was the building of a fort, and the spot
they chose was a furlong or more above St. John's
Bluff, where close to the water was a wide, flat knoll,
raised a few feet above the marsh and the river.[1]
Boats came up the stream with laborers, tents, provisions, cannon, and tools. The engineers marked
out the work in the form of a triangle; and, from the
noble volunteer to the meanest artisan, all lent a

[1] Above St. John's Bluff the shore curves in a semicircle, along
which the water runs in a deep, strong current, which has half cut
away the flat knoll above mentioned, and encroached greatly on the
bluff itself. The formation of the ground, joined to the indications
furnished by Laudonnière and Le Moyne, leave little doubt that the
fort was built on the knoll.

hand to complete it. On the river side the defences were a palisade of timber. On the two other sides were a ditch, and a rampart of fascines, earth, and sods. At each angle was a bastion, in one of which was the magazine. Within was a spacious parade, around it were various buildings for lodging and storage, and a large house with covered galleries was built on the side towards the river for Laudonnière and his officers. In honor of Charles the Ninth the fort was named Fort Caroline.

Meanwhile Satouriona, "lord of all that country," as the narratives style him, was seized with misgivings on learning these proceedings. The work was scarcely begun, and all was din and confusion around the incipient fort, when the startled Frenchmen saw the neighboring height of St. John's swarming with naked warriors. Laudonnière set his men in array, and for a season, pick and spade were dropped for arquebuse and pike. The savage chief descended to the camp. The artist Le Moyne, who saw him, drew his likeness from memory, — a tall, athletic figure, tattooed in token of his rank, plumed, bedecked with strings of beads, and girdled with tinkling pieces of metal which hung from the belt which formed his only garment.[1] He came in regal state, a crowd of warriors around him, and, in advance, a troop of young Indians armed with spears. Twenty musicians followed, blowing hideous discord through pipes of reeds,[2] while he seated himself on the ground "like

[1] Le Moyne, Tabulæ VIII., XI.
[2] Le Moyne, *Brevis Narratio.*

a monkey," as Le Moyne has it in the grave Latin of his *Brevis Narratio*. A council followed, in which broken words were aided by signs and pantomime; and a treaty of alliance was made, Laudonnière renewing his rash promise to aid the chief against his enemies. Satouriona, well pleased, ordered his Indians to help the French in their work. They obeyed with alacrity, and in two days the buildings of the fort were all thatched, after the native fashion, with leaves of the palmetto.

These savages belonged to one of the confederacies into which the native tribes of Florida were divided, and with three of which the French came into contact. The first was that of Satouriona; and the second was that of the people called Thimagoas, who, under a chief named Outina, dwelt in forty villages high up the St. John's. The third was that of the chief, cacique, or paracoussy whom the French called King Potanou, and whose dominions lay among the pine barrens, cypress swamps, and fertile hummocks westward and northwestward of this remarkable river. These three confederacies hated each other, and were constantly at war. Their social state was more advanced than that of the wandering hunter tribes. They were an agricultural people, and around all their villages were fields of maize, beans, and pumpkins. The harvest was gathered into a public granary, and they lived on it during three fourths of the year, dispersing in winter to hunt among the forests.

They were exceedingly well formed; the men, or

the principal among them, were tattooed on the limbs and body, and in summer were nearly naked. Some wore their straight black hair flowing loose to the waist; others gathered it in a knot at the crown of the head. They danced and sang about the scalps of their enemies, like the tribes of the North; and like them they had their "medicine-men," who combined the functions of physicians, sorcerers, and priests. The most prominent feature of their religion was sun-worship.

Their villages were clusters of large dome-shaped huts, framed with poles and thatched with palmetto leaves. In the midst was the dwelling of the chief, much larger than the rest, and sometimes raised on an artificial mound. They were enclosed with palisades, and, strange to say, some of them were approached by wide avenues, artificially graded, and several hundred yards in length. Traces of these may still be seen, as may also the mounds in which the Floridians, like the Hurons and various other tribes, collected at stated intervals the bones of their dead.

Social distinctions were sharply defined among them. Their chiefs, whose office was hereditary, sometimes exercised a power almost absolute. Each village had its chief, subordinate to the grand chief of the confederacy. In the language of the French narratives, they were all kings or lords, vassals of the great monarch Satouriona, Outina, or Potanou. All these tribes are now extinct, and it is difficult to

ascertain with precision their tribal affinities. There
can be no doubt that they were the authors of the
aboriginal remains at present found in various parts
of Florida.

Having nearly finished the fort, Laudonnière declares that he "would not lose the minute of an houre
without employing of the same in some vertuous exercise;" and he therefore sent his lieutenant, Ottigny,
to spy out the secrets of the interior, and to learn,
above all, "what this Thimagoa might be, whereof
the Paracoussy Satouriona had spoken to us so
often." As Laudonnière stood pledged to attack the
Thimagoas, the chief gave Ottigny two Indian guides,
who, says the record, were so eager for the fray that
they seemed as if bound to a wedding feast.

The lazy waters of the St. John's, tinged to coffee-
color by the exudations of the swamps, curled before
the prow of Ottigny's sail-boat as he advanced into
the prolific wilderness which no European eye had
ever yet beheld. By his own reckoning, he sailed
thirty leagues up the river, which would have
brought him to a point not far below Palatka. Here,
more than two centuries later, the Bartrams, father
and son, guided their skiff and kindled their nightly
bivouac-fire; and here, too, roamed Audubon, with
his sketch-book and his gun. It was a paradise for
the hunter and the naturalist. Earth, air, and water
teemed with life, in endless varieties of beauty and
ugliness. A half-tropical forest shadowed the low
shores, where the palmetto and the cabbage palm

mingled with the oak, the maple, the cypress, the liquid-ambar, the laurel, the myrtle, and the broad glistening leaves of the evergreen magnolia. Here was the haunt of bears, wild-cats, lynxes, cougars, and the numberless deer of which they made their prey. In the sedges and the mud the alligator stretched his brutish length; turtles with outstretched necks basked on half-sunken logs; the rattlesnake sunned himself on the sandy bank, and the yet more dangerous moccason lurked under the water-lilies in inlets and sheltered coves. The air and the water were populous as the earth. The river swarmed with fish, from the fierce and restless gar, cased in his horny armor, to the lazy cat-fish in the muddy depths. There were the golden eagle and the white-headed eagle, the gray pelican and the white pelican, the blue heron and the white heron, the egret, the ibis, ducks of various sorts, the whooping crane, the black vulture, and the cormorant; and when at sun-set the voyagers drew their boat upon the strand and built their camp-fire under the arches of the woods, the owls whooped around them all night long, and when morning came the sultry mists that wrapped the river were vocal with the clamor of wild turkeys.

When Ottigny was about twenty leagues from Fort Caroline, his two Indian guides, who were always on the watch, descried three canoes, and in great excitement cried, "Thimagoa! Thimagoa!" As they drew near, one of them snatched up a halberd and the

other a sword, and in their fury they seemed ready
to jump into the water to get at the enemy.   To
their great disgust, Ottigny permitted the Thimagoas
to run their canoes ashore and escape to the woods.
Far from keeping Laudonnière's senseless promise to
fight them, he wished to make them friends; to
which end he now landed with some of his men,
placed a few trinkets in their canoes, and withdrew
to a distance to watch the result.   The fugitives
presently returned, step by step, and allowed the
French to approach them; on which Ottigny asked,
by signs, if they had gold or silver.   They replied
that they had none, but that if he would give them
one of his men they would show him where it was to
be found.   One of the soldiers boldly offered himself
for the venture, and embarked with them.   As,
however, he failed to return according to agreement,
Ottigny, on the next day, followed ten leagues farther
up the stream, and at length had the good luck to
see him approaching in a canoe.   He brought little
or no gold, but reported that he had heard of a certain chief, named Mayrra, marvellously rich, who
lived three days' journey up the river; and with
these welcome tidings Ottigny went back to Fort
Caroline.

A fortnight later, an officer named Vasseur went
up the river to pursue the adventure.   The fever for
gold had seized upon the French.   As the villages of
the Thimagoas lay between them and the imagined
treasures, they shrank from a quarrel, and Laudon-

nière repented already of his promised alliance with Satouriona.

Vasseur was two days' sail from the fort when two Indians hailed him from the shore, inviting him to their dwellings. He accepted their guidance, and presently saw before him the cornfields and palisades of an Indian town. He and his followers were led through the wondering crowd to the lodge of Mollua, the chief, seated in the place of honor, and plentifully regaled with fish and bread. The repast over, Mollua made a speech. He told them that he was one of the forty vassal chiefs of the great Outina, lord of all the Thimagoas, whose warriors wore armor of gold and silver plate. He told them, too, of Potanou, his enemy, "a man cruell in warre;" and of the two kings of the distant Appalachian Mountains, — Onatheaqua and Houstaqua, "great lords and abounding in riches." While thus, with earnest pantomime and broken words, the chief discoursed with his guests, Vasseur, intent and eager, strove to follow his meaning; and no sooner did he hear of these Appalachian treasures than he promised to join Outina in war against the two potentates of the mountains. Mollua, well pleased, promised that each of Outina's vassal chiefs should requite their French allies with a heap of gold and silver two feet high. Thus, while Laudonnière stood pledged to Satouriona, Vasseur made alliance with his mortal enemy.

On his return, he passed a night in the lodge of one of Satouriona's chiefs, who questioned him touching his dealings with the Thimagoas. Vasseur replied that he had set upon them and put them to utter rout. But as the chief, seeming as yet unsatisfied, continued his inquiries, the sergeant François de la Caille drew his sword, and, like Falstaff, re-enacted his deeds of valor, pursuing and thrusting at the imaginary Thimagoas, as they fled before his fury. The chief, at length convinced, led the party to his lodge, and entertained them with a decoction of the herb called Cassina.

Satouriona, elated by Laudonnière's delusive promises of aid, had summoned his so-called vassals to war. Ten chiefs and some five hundred warriors had mustered at his call, and the forest was alive with their bivouacs. When all was ready, Satouriona reminded the French commander of his pledge, and claimed its fulfilment, but got nothing but evasions in return. He stifled his rage, and prepared to go without his fickle ally.

A fire was kindled near the bank of the river, and two large vessels of water were placed beside it. Here Satouriona took his stand, while his chiefs crouched on the grass around him, and the savage visages of his five hundred warriors filled the outer circle, their long hair garnished with feathers, or covered with the heads and skins of wolves, cougars, bears, or eagles. Satouriona, looking towards the country of his enemy, distorted his features into a wild expression of rage and hate; then muttered to himself; then howled an invocation to his god, the

Sun; then besprinkled the assembly with water from
one of the vessels, and, turning the other upon the
fire, suddenly quenched it. "So," he cried, "may
the blood of our enemies be poured out, and their
lives extinguished!" and the concourse gave forth an
explosion of responsive yells, till the shores resounded
with the wolfish din.[1]

The rites over, they set out, and in a few days
returned exulting, with thirteen prisoners and a
number of scalps. These last were hung on a pole
before the royal lodge; and when night came, it
brought with it a pandemonium of dancing and
whooping, drumming and feasting.

A notable scheme entered the brain of Laudonnière.
Resolved, cost what it might, to make a friend of
Outina, he conceived it to be a stroke of policy to
send back to him two of the prisoners. In the morning he sent a soldier to Satouriona to demand them.
The astonished chief gave a flat refusal, adding that
he owed the French no favors, for they had shame-
fully broken faith with him. On this, Laudonnière,
at the head of twenty soldiers, proceeded to the
Indian town, placed a guard at the opening of the
great lodge, entered with his arquebusiers, and seated
himself without ceremony in the highest place. Here,
to show his displeasure, he remained in silence for
half an hour. At length he spoke, renewing his
demand. For some moments Satouriona made no
reply; then he coldly observed that the sight of so

---

[1] Le Moyne makes the scene the subject of one of his pictures.

many armed men had frightened the prisoners away. Laudonnière grew peremptory, when the chief's son, Athore, went out, and presently returned with the two Indians, whom the French led back to Fort Caroline.[1]

Satouriona, says Laudonnière, "was wonderfully offended with his bravado, and bethought himselfe by all meanes how he might be revenged of us." He dissembled for the time, and presently sent three of his followers to the fort with a gift of pumpkins; though under this show of good-will the outrage rankled in his breast, and he never forgave it. The French had been unfortunate in their dealings with the Indians. They had alienated old friends in vain attempts to make new ones.

Vasseur, with the Swiss ensign Arlac,[2] a sergeant, and ten soldiers, went up the river early in September to carry back the two prisoners to Outina. Laudonnière declares that they sailed eighty leagues, which would have carried them far above Lake Monroe; but it is certain that his reckoning is grossly exaggerated. Their boat crawled up the lazy St. John's, no longer a broad lake-like expanse, but a narrow and tortuous stream, winding between swampy forests, or through the vast savanna, a verdant sea of bulrushes and grass. At length they came to a village called Mayarqua, and thence, with the help of their oars, made their way to another cluster of wigwams, appar-

[1] Laudonnière in Hakluyt, III. 396.
[2] So written by Laudonnière. The true name is probably **Erlach**.

ently on a branch of the main river.   Here they found
Outina himself, whom, prepossessed with ideas of
feudality, they regarded as the suzerain of a host of
subordinate lords and princes, ruling over the surrounding swamps and pine barrens.   Outina grate-
fully received the two prisoners whom Laudonnière
had sent to propitiate him, feasted the wonderful
strangers, and invited them to join him on a raid
against his rival, Potanou.   Laudonnière had promised
to join Satouriona against Outina, and Vasseur now
promised to join Outina against Potanou, the hope of
finding gold being in both cases the source of this
impolitic compliance.   Vasseur went back to Fort
Caroline with five of the men, and left Arlac with
the remaining five to fight the battles of Outina.

The warriors mustered to the number of some two
hundred, and the combined force of white men and
red took up their march.   The wilderness through
which they passed has not yet quite lost its characteristic features, — the bewildering monotony of the
pine barrens, with their myriads of bare gray trunks
and their canopy of perennial green, through which
a scorching sun throws spots and streaks of yellow
light, here on an undergrowth of dwarf palmetto,
and there on dry sands half hidden by tufted wire-
grass, and dotted with the little mounds that mark
the burrows of the gopher; or those oases in the
desert, the "hummocks," with their wild, redundant
vegetation, their entanglement of trees, bushes, and
vines, their scent of flowers and song of birds; or the

broad sunshine of the savanna, where they waded to the neck in grass; or the deep swamp, where, out of the black and root-encumbered slough, rise the huge buttressed trunks of the Southern cypress, the gray Spanish moss drooping from every bough and twig, wrapping its victims like a drapery of tattered cobwebs, and slowly draining away their life, for even plants devour each other, and play their silent parts in the universal tragedy of nature.

The allies held their way through forest, savanna, and swamp, with Outina's Indians in the front, till they neared the hostile villages, when the modest warriors fell to the rear, and yielded the post of honor to the Frenchmen.

An open country lay before them, with rough fields of maize, beans, and pumpkins, and the palisades of an Indian town. Their approach was seen, and the warriors of Potanou swarmed out to meet them; but the sight of the bearded strangers, the flash and report of the fire-arms, and the fall of their foremost chief, shot through the brain by Arlac, filled them with consternation, and they fled within their defences. Pursuers and pursued entered pell-mell together. The place was pillaged and burned, its inmates captured or killed, and the victors returned triumphant.

CHAPTER V.

1564, 1565.

CONSPIRACY.

DISCONTENT. — PLOT OF LA ROQUETTE. — PIRATICAL EXCURSION. — SEDITION. — ILLNESS OF LAUDONNIÈRE. — OUTBREAK OF THE MUTINY. — BUCCANEERING. — ORDER RESTORED.

In the little world of Fort Caroline, a miniature France, cliques and parties, conspiracy and sedition, were fast stirring into life. Hopes had been dashed, and wild expectations had come to naught. The adventurers had found, not conquest and gold, but a dull exile in a petty fort by a hot and sickly river, with hard labor, bad fare, prospective famine, and nothing to break the weary sameness but some passing canoe or floating alligator. Gathered in knots, they nursed each other's wrath, and inveighed against the commandant. Why are we put on half-rations, when he told us that provision should be made for a full year? Where are the reinforcements and supplies that he said should follow us from France? And why is he always closeted with Ottigny, Arlac, and this and that favorite, when we, men of blood as good as theirs, cannot gain his ear for a moment?

The young nobles, of whom there were many, were volunteers, who had paid their own expenses in expectation of a golden harvest, and they chafed in impatience and disgust. The religious element in the colony — unlike the former Huguenot emigration to Brazil — was evidently subordinate. The adven-turers thought more of their fortunes than of their faith; yet there were not a few earnest enough in the doctrine of Geneva to complain loudly and bitterly that no ministers had been sent with them. The burden of all grievances was thrown upon Laudonnière, whose greatest errors seem to have arisen from weakness and a lack of judgment, — fatal defects in his position.

The growing discontent was brought to a partial head by one La Roquette, who gave out that, high up the river, he had discovered by magic a mine of gold and silver, which would give each of them a share of ten thousand crowns, besides fifteen hundred thousand for the King. But for Laudonnière, he said, their fortunes would all be made. He found an ally in a gentleman named Genre, one of Laudonnière's confidants, who, while still professing fast adherence to his interests, is charged by him with plotting against his life. "This Genre," he says, "secretly enfourmed the Souldiers that were already suborned by La Roquette, that I would deprive them of this great gaine, in that I did set them dayly on worke, not sending them on every side to discover the Countreys; therefore that it were a good deede to dispatch mee out of the way, and to choose another Captaine in my place." The soldiers listened too

well.   They made a flag of an old shirt, which they
carried with them to the rampart when they went to
their work, at the same time wearing their arms; and,
pursues Laudonnière, "these gentle Souldiers did the
same for none other ende but to have killed mee and
my Lieutenant also, if by chance I had given them
any hard speeches." About this time, overheating
himself, he fell ill, and was confined to his quarters.
On this, Genre made advances to the apothecary,
urging him to put arsenic into his medicine; but
the apothecary shrugged his shoulders. They next
devised a scheme to blow him up by hiding a keg of
gunpowder under his bed; but here, too, they failed.
Hints of Genre's machinations reaching the ears of
Laudonnière, the culprit fled to the woods, whence
he wrote repentant letters, with full confession, to
his commander.

Two of the ships meanwhile returned to France,
— the third, the "Breton," remaining at anchor opposite the fort. The malcontents took the opportunity
to send home charges against Laudonnière of pecula-
tion, favoritism, and tyranny.[1]

On the fourth of September, Captain Bourdet,
apparently a private adventurer, had arrived from
France with a small vessel. When he returned,
about the tenth of November, Laudonnière persuaded
him to carry home seven or eight of the malcontent
soldiers. Bourdet left some of his sailors in their

    [1] Barcia, *Ensayo Cronologico*, 53; Laudonnière in Hakluyt, III. 400;
Basanier, 61.

place. The exchange proved most disastrous. These pirates joined with others whom they had won over, stole Laudonnière's two pinnaces, and set forth on a plundering excursion to the West Indies. They took a small Spanish vessel off the coast of Cuba, but were soon compelled by famine to put into Havana and give themselves up. Here, to make their peace with the authorities, they told all they knew of the position and purposes of their countrymen at Fort Caroline, and thus was forged the thunderbolt soon to be hurled against the wretched little colony.

On a Sunday morning, François de la Caille[1] came to Laudonnière's quarters, and, in the name of the whole company, requested him to come to the parade-ground. He complied, and issuing forth, his insepa-rable Ottigny at his side, he saw some thirty of his officers, soldiers, and gentlemen volunteers waiting before the building with fixed and sombre counte-nances. La Caille, advancing, begged leave to read, in behalf of the rest, a paper which he held in his hand. It opened with protestations of duty and obe-dience; next came complaints of hard work, starva-tion, and broken promises, and a request that the petitioners should be allowed to embark in the vessel lying in the river, and cruise along the Spanish Main, in order to procure provisions by purchase " or other-

---

[1] La Caille, as before mentioned, was Laudonnière's sergeant. The feudal rank of sergeant, it will be remembered, was widely different from the modern grade so named, and was held by men of noble birth. Le Moyne calls La Caille " Captain."

wise." [1]   In short, the flower of the company wished
to turn buccaneers.

Laudonnière refused, but assured them that, as
soon as the defences of the fort should be completed,
a search should be begun in earnest for the Appalachian gold mine, and that meanwhile two small
vessels then building on the river should be sent
along the coast to barter for provisions with the
Indians.   With this answer they were forced to content themselves; but the fermentation continued, and
the plot thickened.   Their spokesman, La Caille,
however, seeing whither the affair tended, broke with
them, and, except Ottigny, Vasseur, and the brave
Swiss Arlac, was the only officer who held to his
duty.

A severe illness again seized Laudonnière, and confined him to his bed.   Improving their advantage,
the malcontents gained over nearly all the best soldiers
in the fort.   The ringleader was one Fourneaux, a
man of good birth, but whom Le Moyne calls an avaricious hypocrite.   He drew up a paper, to which
sixty-six names were signed.   La Caille boldly opposed
the conspirators, and they resolved to kill him.   His
room-mate, Le Moyne, who had also refused to sign,
received a hint of the design from a friend; upon
which he warned La Caille, who escaped to the
woods.   It was late in the night.   Fourneaux, with
twenty men armed to the teeth, knocked fiercely at
the commandant's door.   Forcing an entrance, they

[1] Le Moyne, *Brevis Narratio*.

wounded a gentleman who opposed them, and crowded around the sick man's bed. Fourneaux, armed with steel cap and cuirass, held his arquebuse to Laudonnière's throat, and demanded leave to go on a cruise among the Spanish islands. The latter kept his presence of mind, and remonstrated with some firmness; on which, with oaths and menaces, they dragged him from his bed, put him in fetters, carried him out to the gate of the fort, placed him in a boat, and rowed him to the ship anchored in the river.

Two other gangs at the same time visited Ottigny and Arlac, whom they disarmed, and ordered to keep their rooms till the night following, on pain of death. Smaller parties were busied, meanwhile, in disarming all the loyal soldiers. The fort was completely in the hands of the conspirators. Fourneaux drew up a commission for his meditated West India cruise, which he required Laudonnière to sign. The sick commandant, imprisoned in the ship with one attendant, at first refused; but receiving a message from the mutineers, that, if he did not comply, they would come on board and cut his throat, he at length yielded.

The buccaneers now bestirred themselves to finish the two small vessels on which the carpenters had been for some time at work. In a fortnight they were ready for sea, armed and provided with the King's cannon, munitions, and stores. Trenchant, an excellent pilot, was forced to join the party. Their favorite object was the plunder of a certain church on one of the Spanish islands, which they proposed to assail during the midnight mass of Christmas, whereby a triple end would be achieved, — first, a rich booty; secondly, the punishment of idolatry; thirdly, vengeance on the arch-enemies of their party and their faith. They set sail on the eighth of December, taunting those who remained, calling them greenhorns, and threatening condign punishment if, on their triumphant return, they should be refused free entrance to the fort.[1]

They were no sooner gone than the unfortunate Laudonnière was gladdened in his solitude by the approach of his fast friends Ottigny and Arlac, who conveyed him to the fort and reinstated him. The entire command was reorganized, and new officers appointed. The colony was wofully depleted; but the bad blood had been drawn off, and thenceforth all internal danger was at an end. In finishing the fort, in building two new vessels to replace those of which they had been robbed, and in various intercourse with the tribes far and near, the weeks passed until the twenty-fifth of March, when an Indian came in with the tidings that a vessel was hovering off the coast. Laudonnière sent to reconnoitre. The stranger lay anchored at the mouth of the river. She was a Spanish brigantine, manned by the returning mutineers, starving, downcast, and anxious to make terms. Yet, as their posture seemed not wholly

---

[1] Le Moyne, *Brevis Narratio.* Compare Laudonnière in Basanier, fol. 63–66.

pacific, Laudonnière sent down La Caille, with thirty soldiers concealed at the bottom of his little vessel. Seeing only two or three on deck, the pirates allowed her to come alongside; when, to their amazement, they were boarded and taken before they could snatch their arms. Discomfited, woebegone, and drunk, they were landed under a guard. Their story was soon told. Fortune had flattered them at the outset, and on the coast of Cuba they took a brigantine laden with wine and stores. Embarking in her, they next fell in with a caravel, which also they captured. Landing at a village in Jamaica, they plundered and caroused for a week, and had hardly re-embarked when they met a small vessel having on board the governor of the island.[1] She made a desperate fight, but was taken at last, and with her a rich booty. They thought to put the governor to ransom; but the astute official deceived them, and, on pretence of negotiating for the sum demanded, — together with "four or six parrots, and as many monkeys of the sort called sanguins, which are very beautiful," and for which his captors had also bargained, — contrived to send instructions to his wife. Hence it happened that at daybreak three armed vessels fell upon them, retook the prize, and captured or killed all the pirates but twenty-six, who, cutting the moorings of their brigantine, fled out to sea. Among these was the ringleader Fourneaux, and also the pilot Trenchant,

---

[1] Laudonnière in Basanier, fol. 66. Le Moyne says that it was the governor of Havana.

who, eager to return to Fort Caroline, whence he had been forcibly taken, succeeded during the night in bringing the vessel to the coast of Florida. Great were the wrath and consternation of the pirates when they saw their dilemma; for, having no provisions, they must either starve or seek succor at the fort. They chose the latter course, and bore away for the St. John's. A few casks of Spanish wine yet remained, and nobles and soldiers, fraternizing in the common peril of a halter, joined in a last carouse. As the wine mounted to their heads, in the mirth of drink and desperation, they enacted their own trial. One personated the judge, another the commandant; witnesses were called, with arguments and speeches on either side.

"Say what you like," said one of them, after hearing the counsel for the defence; "but if Laudonnière does not hang us all, I will never call him an honest man."

They had some hope of getting provisions from the Indians at the mouth of the river, and then putting to sea again; but this was frustrated by La Caille's sudden attack. A court-martial was called near Fort Caroline, and all were found guilty. Fourneaux and three others were sentenced to be hanged.

"Comrades," said one of the condemned, appealing to the soldiers, "will you stand by and see us butchered?"

"These," retorted Laudonnière, "are no comrades of mutineers and rebels."

At the request of his followers, however, he commuted the sentence to shooting.

A file of men, a rattling volley, and the debt of justice was paid.   The bodies were hanged on gibbets, at the river's mouth, and order reigned at Fort Caroline.[1]

---

[1] The above is from Le Moyne and Laudonnière, who agree in essential points, but differ in a few details.   The artist criticises the commandant freely.   Compare Hawkins in Hakluyt, III. 614.

CHAPTER VI.

1564, 1565.

FAMINE. — WAR. — SUCCOR.

La Roche Ferrière. — Pierre Gambie. — The King of Calos.
— Ottigny's Expedition. — Starvation. — Efforts to escape
from Florida. — Indians unfriendly. — Seizure of Outina.
— Attempts to extort Ransom. — Ambuscade. — Battle. —
Desperation of the French. — Sir John Hawkins relieves
them. — Ribaut brings Reinforcements. — Arrival of the
Spaniards.

WHILE the mutiny was brewing, one La Roche
Ferrière had been sent out as an agent or emissary
among the more distant tribes. Sagacious, bold, and
restless, he pushed his way from town to town, and
pretended to have reached the mysterious mountains
of Appalache. He sent to the fort mantles woven
with feathers, quivers covered with choice furs,
arrows tipped with gold, wedges of a green stone like
beryl or emerald, and other trophies of his wander-
ings. A gentleman named Grotaut took up the
quest, and penetrated to the dominions of Hostaqua,
who, it was pretended, could muster three or four
thousand warriors, and who promised, with the aid of
a hundred arquebusiers, to conquer all the kings of
the adjacent mountains, and subject them and their
gold mines to the rule of the French. A humbler

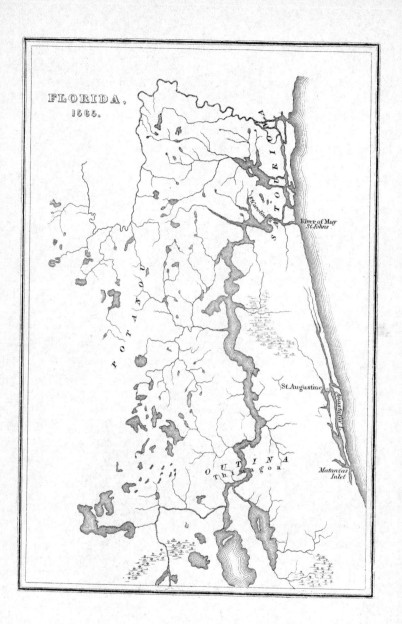

FLORIDA,
1565.

Carolina

S. TOURIS

River of May
St. Johns

POTAROU

St. Augustine

Anastatia I.

OUTINA
Thimagoa

Matanzas
Inlet

adventurer was Pierre Gambie, a robust and daring youth, who had been brought up in the household of Coligny, and was now a soldier under Laudonnière. The latter gave him leave to trade with the Indians, — a privilege which he used so well that he grew rich with his traffic, became prime favorite with the chief of the island of Edelano, married his daughter, and, in his absence, reigned in his stead. But, as his sway verged towards despotism, his subjects took offence, and split his head with a hatchet.

During the winter, Indians from the neighborhood of Cape Canaveral brought to the fort two Spaniards, wrecked fifteen years before on the southwestern extremity of the peninsula. They were clothed like the Indians, — in other words, were not clothed at all, — and their uncut hair streamed loose down their backs. They brought strange tales of those among whom they had dwelt. They told of the King of Calos, on whose domains they had been wrecked, a chief mighty in stature and in power. In one of his villages was a pit, six feet deep and as wide as a hogshead, filled with treasure gathered from Spanish wrecks on adjacent reefs and keys. The monarch was a priest too, and a magician, with power over the elements. Each year he withdrew from the public gaze to hold converse in secret with supernal or infernal powers; and each year he sacrificed to his gods one of the Spaniards whom the fortune of the sea had cast upon his shores. The name of the tribe is preserved in that of the river Caloosa. In close league with him was the mighty Oathcaqua, dwelling near Cape Canaveral, who gave his daughter, a maiden of wondrous beauty, in marriage to his great ally.   But as the bride with her bridesmaids was journeying towards Calos, escorted by a chosen band, they were assailed by a wild and warlike race, inhabitants of an island called Sarrope, in the midst of a lake, who put the warriors to flight, bore the maidens captive to their watery fastness, espoused them all, and, we are assured, "loved them above all measure." [1]

Outina, taught by Arlac the efficacy of the French fire-arms, begged for ten arquebusiers to aid him on a new raid among the villages of Potanou, — again alluring his greedy allies by the assurance, that, thus reinforced, he would conquer for them a free access to the phantom gold mines of Appalache.   Ottigny set forth on this fool's errand with thrice the force demanded.   Three hundred Thimagoas and thirty Frenchmen took up their march through the pine barrens.   Outina's conjurer was of the number, and had wellnigh ruined the enterprise.   Kneeling on Ottigny's shield, that he might not touch the earth, with hideous grimaces, howlings, and contortions, he wrought himself into a prophetic frenzy, and proclaimed to the astounded warriors that to advance farther would be destruction. [2]   Outina was for instant

[1] Laudonnière in Hakluyt, III. 406.   Brinton, *Floridian Peninsula*, thinks there is truth in the story, and that Lake Weir, in Marion County, is the Lake of Sarrope.   I give these romantic tales as I find them.

[2] This scene is the subject of Plate XII. of Le Moyne.

R. Holata Outina.

OUTINA AND HIS CONJURER.

retreat, but Ottigny's sarcasms shamed him into a show of courage. Again they moved forward, and soon encountered Potanou with all his host.[1] The arquebuse did its work, — panic, slaughter, and a plentiful harvest of scalps. But no persuasion could induce Outina to follow up his victory. He went home to dance round his trophies, and the French returned disgusted to Fort Caroline.

And now, in ample measure, the French began to reap the harvest of their folly. Conquest, gold, and military occupation had alone been their aims. Not a rood of ground had been stirred with the spade. Their stores were consumed, and the expected supplies had not come. The Indians, too, were hostile. Satouriona hated them as allies of his enemies; and his tribesmen, robbed and maltreated by the lawless soldiers, exulted in their miseries. Yet in these, their dark and subtle neighbors, was their only hope.

May-day came, the third anniversary of the day when Ribaut and his companions, full of delighted anticipation, had first explored the flowery borders of the St. John's. The contrast was deplorable; for within the precinct of Fort Caroline a homesick, squalid band, dejected and worn, dragged their shrunken limbs about the sun-scorched area, or lay

---

[1] Le Moyne drew a picture of the fight (Plate XIII.). In the foreground Ottigny is engaged in single combat with a gigantic savage, who, with club upheaved, aims a deadly stroke at the plumed helmet of his foe; but the latter, with target raised to guard his head, darts under the arms of the naked Goliath, and transfixes him with his sword.

stretched in listless wretchedness under the shade of
the barracks.   Some were digging roots in the forest,
or gathering a kind of sorrel upon the meadows.   If
they had had any skill in hunting and fishing, the
river and the woods would have supplied their needs;
but in this point, as in others, they were lamentably
unfit for the work they had taken in hand.   "Our
miserie," says Laudonnière, "was so great that one
was found that gathered up all the fish-bones that he
could finde, which he dried and beate into powder to
make bread thereof.   The effects of this hideous
famine appeared incontinently among us, for our
bones eftsoones beganne to cleave so neere unto the
skinne, that the most part of the souldiers had their
skinnes pierced thorow with them in many partes of
their bodies."   Yet, giddy with weakness, they
dragged themselves in turn to the top of St. John's
Bluff, straining their eyes across the sea to descry the
anxiously expected sail.

Had Coligny left them to perish? or had some new
tempest of calamity, let loose upon France, drowned
the memory of their exile?   In vain the watchman
on the hill surveyed the solitude of waters.   A deep
dejection fell upon them, — a dejection that would
have sunk to despair could their eyes have pierced
the future.

The Indians had left the neighborhood, but from
time to time brought in meagre supplies of fish, which
they sold to the famished soldiers at exorbitant prices.
Lest they should pay the penalty of their extortion,

they would not enter the fort, but lay in their canoes in the river, beyond gunshot, waiting for their customers to come out to them. "Oftentimes," says Laudonnière, "our poor soldiers were constrained to give away the very shirts from their backs to get one fish. If at any time they shewed unto the savages the excessive price which they tooke, these villaines would answere them roughly and churlishly: If thou make so great account of thy marchandise, eat it, and we will eat our fish: then fell they out a laughing, and mocked us with open throat."

The spring wore away, and no relief appeared. One thought now engrossed the colonists, that of return to France. Vasseur's ship, the "Breton," still remained in the river, and they had also the Spanish brigantine brought by the mutineers. But these vessels were insufficient, and they prepared to build a new one. The energy of reviving hope lent new life to their exhausted frames. Some gathered pitch in the pine forests; some made charcoal; some cut and sawed timber. The maize began to ripen, and this brought some relief; but the Indians, exasperated and greedy, sold it with reluctance, and murdered two half-famished Frenchmen who gathered a handful in the fields.

The colonists applied to Outina, who owed them two victories. The result was a churlish message and a niggardly supply of corn, coupled with an invitation to aid him against an insurgent chief, one Astina, the plunder of whose villages would yield an

ample supply.   The offer was accepted.   Ottigny and
Vasseur set out, but were grossly deceived, led
against a different enemy, and sent back empty-
handed and half-starved.

They returned to the fort, in the words of Laudonnière, "angry and pricked deepely to the quicke for
being so mocked," and, joined by all their comrades,
fiercely demanded to be led against Outina, to seize
him, punish his insolence, and extort from his fears
the supplies which could not be looked for from his
gratitude.   The commandant was forced to comply.
Those who could bear the weight of their armor put
it on, embarked, to the number of fifty, in two
barges, and sailed up the river under Laudonnière
himself.   Having reached Outina's landing, they
marched inland, entered his village, surrounded his
mud-plastered palace, seized him amid the yells and
howlings of his subjects, and led him prisoner to their
boats.   Here, anchored in mid-stream, they demanded
a supply of corn and beans as the price of his ransom.

The alarm spread.   Excited warriors, bedaubed
with red, came thronging from all his villages.   The
forest along the shore was full of them; and the wife
of the chief, followed by all the women of the place,
uttered moans and outcries from the strand.   Yet no
ransom was offered, since, reasoning from their own
instincts, they never doubted that, after the price was
paid, the captive would be put to death.

Laudonnière waited two days, and then descended
the river with his prisoner.   In a rude chamber of

Fort Caroline the sentinel stood his guard, pike in hand, while before him crouched the captive chief, mute, impassive, and brooding on his woes.   His old enemy, Satouriona, keen as a hound on the scent of prey, tried, by great offers, to bribe Laudonnière to give Outina into his hands; but the French captain refused, treated his prisoner kindly, and assured him of immediate freedom on payment of the ransom.

Meanwhile his captivity was bringing grievous affliction on his tribesmen; for, despairing of his return, they mustered for the election of a new chief.   Party strife ran high.   Some were for a boy, his son, and some for an ambitious kinsman.   Outina chafed in his prison on learning these dissensions; and, eager to convince his over-hasty subjects that their chief still lived, he was so profuse of promises that he was again embarked and carried up the river.

At no great distance from Lake George, a small affluent of the St. John's gave access by water to a point within six French leagues of Outina's principal town.   The two barges, crowded with soldiers, and bearing also the captive Outina, rowed up this little stream.   Indians awaited them at the landing, with gifts of bread, beans, and fish, and piteous prayers for their chief, upon whose liberation they promised an ample supply of corn.   As they were deaf to all other terms, Laudonnière yielded, released his prisoner, and received in his place two hostages, who were fast bound in the boats. Ottigny and Arlac, with a strong detachment of arquebusiers, went to receive the promised supplies, for which, from the first, full payment in merchandise had been offered. On their arrival at the village, they filed into the great central lodge, within whose dusky precincts were gathered the magnates of the tribe. Council-chamber, forum, banquet-hall, and dancing-hall all in one, the spacious structure could hold half the population. Here the French made their abode. With armor buckled, and arquebuse matches lighted, they watched with anxious eyes the strange, dim scene, half revealed by the daylight that streamed down through the hole at the apex of the roof. Tall, dark forms stalked to and fro, with quivers at their backs, and bows and arrows in their hands, while groups, crouched in the shadow beyond, eyed the hated guests with inscrutable visages, and malignant, sidelong eyes. Corn came in slowly, but warriors mustered fast. The village without was full of them. The French officers grew anxious, and urged the chiefs to greater alacrity in collecting the promised ransom. The answer boded no good: "Our women are afraid when they see the matches of your guns burning. Put them out, and they will bring the corn faster."

Outina was nowhere to be seen. At length they learned that he was in one of the small huts adjacent. Several of the officers went to him, complaining of the slow payment of his ransom. The kindness of his captors at Fort Caroline seemed to have won his heart. He replied, that such was the rage of his subjects that he could no longer control them; that

the French were in danger; and that he had seen
arrows stuck in the ground by the side of the path,
in token that war was declared.   The peril was thickening hourly, and Ottigny resolved to regain the
boats while there was yet time.

On the twenty-seventh of July, at nine in the
morning, he set his men in order.   Each shouldering
a sack of corn, they marched through the rows of
huts that surrounded the great lodge, and out betwixt
the overlapping extremities of the palisade that
encircled the town.   Before them stretched a wide
avenue, three or four hundred paces long, flanked by
a natural growth of trees, — one of those curious
monuments of native industry to which allusion has
already been made.[1]   Here Ottigny halted and formed
his line of march.   Arlac, with eight matchlock men,
was sent in advance, and flanking parties were thrown
into the woods on either side.   Ottigny told his
soldiers that, if the Indians meant to attack them,
they were probably in ambush at the other end of the
avenue.   He was right.   As Arlac's party reached
the spot, the whole pack gave tongue at once.   The
war-whoop rose, and a tempest of stone-headed arrows
clattered against the breast-plates of the French, or,
scorching like fire, tore through their unprotected
limbs.   They stood firm, and sent back their shot so
steadily that several of the assailants were laid dead,
and the rest, two or three hundred in number, **gave**
way as Ottigny came up with his men.

[1] See *ante*, p. 58.

They moved on for a quarter of a mile through a country, as it seems, comparatively open, when again the war-cry pealed in front, and three hundred savages bounded to the assault. Their whoops were echoed from the rear. It was the party whom Arlac had just repulsed, and who, leaping and showering their arrows, were rushing on again with a ferocity restrained only by their lack of courage. There was no panic among the French. The men threw down their bags of corn, and took to their weapons. They blew their matches, and, under two excellent officers, stood well to their work. The Indians, on their part, showed good discipline after their fashion, and were perfectly under the control of their chiefs. With cries that imitated the yell of owls, the scream of cougars, and the howl of wolves, they ran up in successive bands, let fly their arrows, and instantly fell back, giving place to others. At the sight of the levelled arquebuse, they dropped flat on the ground. Whenever the French charged upon them, sword in hand, they fled through the woods like foxes; and whenever the march was resumed, the arrows were showering again upon the flanks and rear of the retiring band. As they fell, the soldiers picked them up and broke them. Thus, beset with swarming savages, the handful of Frenchmen pushed slowly onward, fighting as they went.

The Indians gradually drew off, and the forest was silent again. Two of the French had been killed and twenty-two wounded, several so severely that they

were supported to the boats with the utmost difficulty.   Of the corn, two bags only had been brought
off.

Famine and desperation now reigned at Fort
Caroline.   The Indians had killed two of the carpenters; hence long delay in the finishing of the new
ship.   They would not wait, but resolved to put to
sea in the "Breton" and the brigantine.   The problem
was to find food for the voyage; for now, in their
extremity, they roasted and ate snakes, a delicacy in
which the neighborhood abounded.

On the third of August, Laudonnière, perturbed
and oppressed, was walking on the hill, when, looking seaward, he saw a sight that sent a thrill through
his exhausted frame.   A great ship was standing
towards the river's mouth.   Then another came in
sight, and another, and another.   He despatched a
messenger with the tidings to the fort below.   The
languid forms of his sick and despairing men rose
and danced for joy, and voices shrill with weakness
joined in wild laughter and acclamation, insomuch,
he says, "that one would have thought them to bee
out of their wittes."

A doubt soon mingled with their joy.   Who were
the strangers?   Were they the friends so long hoped
for in vain? or were they Spaniards, their dreaded
enemies?   They were neither.   The foremost ship
was a stately one, of seven hundred tons, a great
burden at that day.   She was named the "Jesus;"
and with her were three smaller vessels, the "Solo-

mon," the "Tiger," and the "Swallow." Their commander was "a right worshipful and valiant knight," — for so the record styles him, — a pious man and a prudent, to judge him by the orders he gave his crew when, ten months before, he sailed out of Plymouth: "Serve God daily, love one another, preserve your victuals, beware of fire, and keepe good companie." Nor were the crew unworthy the graces of their chief; for the devout chronicler of the voyage ascribes their deliverance from the perils of the sea to "the Almightie God, who never suffereth his Elect to perish."

Who then were they, this chosen band, serenely conscious of a special Providential care? They were the pioneers of that detested traffic destined to inoculate with its infection nations yet unborn, the parent of discord and death, filling half a continent with the tramp of armies and the clash of fratricidal swords. Their chief was Sir John Hawkins, father of the English slave-trade.

He had been to the coast of Guinea, where he bought and kidnapped a cargo of slaves. These he had sold to the jealous Spaniards of Hispaniola, forcing them, with sword, matchlock, and culverin, to grant him free trade, and then to sign testimonials that he had borne himself as became a peaceful merchant. Prospering greatly by this summary commerce, but distressed by the want of water, he had put into the River of May to obtain a supply.

Among the rugged heroes of the British marine,

ÆTATIS SVÆ LVIII
A DNI 1591

SIR JOHN HAWKINS.

Sir John stood in the front rank, and along with
Drake, his relative, is extolled as "a man borne for
the honour of the English name. . . . Neither did
the West of England yeeld such an Indian Neptunian
paire as were these two Ocean peeres, Hawkins and
Drake." So writes the old chronicler, Purchas,
and all England was of his thinking. A hardy and
skilful seaman, a bold fighter, a loyal friend and a
stern enemy, overbearing towards equals, but kind,
in his bluff way, to those beneath him, rude in
speech, somewhat crafty withal and avaricious, he
buffeted his way to riches and fame, and died at last
full of years and honor. As for the abject humanity
stowed between the reeking decks of the ship "Jesus,"
they were merely in his eyes so many black cattle
tethered for the market.[1]

Hawkins came up the river in a pinnace, and
landed at Fort Caroline, accompanied, says Laudon-

[1] For Hawkins, see the three narratives in Hakluyt, III. 594; Purchas, IV. 1177; Stow, *Chron.*, 807; *Biog. Britan.*, Art. *Hawkins;*
Anderson, *History of Commerce*, I. 400.

He was not knighted until after the voyage of 1564–65; hence there
is an anachronism in the text. As he was held "to have opened a new
trade," he was entitled to bear as his crest a "Moor" or negro, bound
with a cord. In Fairbairn's *Crests of Great Britain and Ireland,* where
it is figured, it is described, not as a negro, but as a "naked man." In
Burke's *Landed Gentry,* it is said that Sir John obtained it in honor of
a great victory over the Moors! His only African victories were in
kidnapping raids on negro villages. In *Letters on Certain Passages in
the Life of Sir John Hawkins,* the coat is engraved in detail. The
"demi-Moor" has the thick lips, the flat nose, and the wool of the
unequivocal negro.

Sir John became Treasurer of the Royal Navy and Rear-Admiral,
and founded a marine hospital at Chatham.

nière, "with gentlemen honorably apparelled, yet unarmed." Between the Huguenots and the English Puritans there was a double tie of sympathy. Both hated priests, and both hated Spaniards. Wakening from their apathetic misery, the starveling garrison hailed him as a deliverer. Yet Hawkins secretly rejoiced when he learned their purpose to abandon Florida; for although, not to tempt his cupidity, they hid from him the secret of their Appalachian gold mine, he coveted for his royal mistress the possession of this rich domain. He shook his head, however, when he saw the vessels in which they proposed to embark, and offered them all a free passage to France in his own ships. This, from obvious motives of honor and prudence, Laudonnière declined, upon which Hawkins offered to lend or sell to him one of his smaller vessels.

Laudonnière hesitated, and hereupon arose a great clamor. A mob of soldiers and artisans beset his chamber, threatening loudly to desert him, and take passage with Hawkins, unless the offer were accepted. The commandant accordingly resolved to buy the vessel. The generous slaver, whose reputed avarice nowhere appears in the transaction, desired him to set his own price; and, in place of money, took the cannon of the fort, with other articles now useless to their late owners. He sent them, too, a gift of wine and biscuit, and supplied them with provisions for the voyage, receiving in payment Laudonnière's note; "for which," adds the latter, "untill this present I am indebted to him." With a friendly leave-taking, he returned to his ships and stood out to sea, leaving golden opinions among the grateful inmates of Fort Caroline.

Before the English top-sails had sunk beneath the horizon, the colonists bestirred themselves to depart. In a few days their preparations were made. They waited only for a fair wind. It was long in coming, and meanwhile their troubled fortunes assumed a new phase.

On the twenty-eighth of August, the two captains Vasseur and Verdier came in with tidings of an approaching squadron. Again the fort was wild with excitement. Friends or foes, French or Spaniards, succor or death, — betwixt these were their hopes and fears divided. On the following morning, they saw seven barges rowing up the river, bristling with weapons, and crowded with men in armor. The sentries on the bluff challenged, and received no answer. One of them fired at the advancing boats, and still there was no response. Laudonnière was almost defenceless. He had given his heavier cannon to Hawkins, and only two field-pieces were left. They were levelled at the foremost boats, and the word to fire was about to be given, when a voice from among the strangers called out that they were French, commanded by Jean Ribaut.

At the eleventh hour, the long looked for succors were come. Ribaut had been commissioned to sail with seven ships for Florida. A disorderly concourse of disbanded soldiers, mixed with artisans and their families, and young nobles weary of a two years' peace, were mustered at the port of Dieppe, and embarked, to the number of three hundred men, bearing with them all things thought necessary to a prosperous colony.

No longer in dread of the Spaniards, the colonists saluted the new-comers with the cannon by which a moment before they had hoped to blow them out of the water. Laudonnière issued from his stronghold to welcome them, and regaled them with what cheer he could. Ribaut was present, conspicuous by his long beard, an astonishment to the Indians; and here, too, were officers, old friends of Laudonnière. Why, then, had they approached in the attitude of enemies? The mystery was soon explained; for they expressed to the commandant their pleasure at finding that the charges made against him had proved false. He begged to know more; on which Ribaut, taking him aside, told him that the returning ships had brought home letters filled with accusations of arrogance, tyranny, cruelty, and a purpose of establishing an independent command, — accusations which he now saw to be unfounded, but which had been the occasion of his unusual and startling precaution. He gave him, too, a letter from Admiral Coligny. In brief but courteous terms, it required him to resign his command, and requested his return to France to clear his name from the imputations cast upon it.[1]

1 See the letter in Basanier, 102.

Ribaut warmly urged him to remain; but Laudonnière declined his friendly proposals.

Worn in body and mind, mortified and wounded, he soon fell ill again. A peasant woman attended him, who was brought over, he says, to nurse the sick and take charge of the poultry, and of whom Le Moyne also speaks as a servant, but who had been made the occasion of additional charges against him, most offensive to the austere Admiral.

Stores were landed, tents were pitched, women and children were sent on shore, feathered Indians mingled in the throng, and the borders of the River of May swarmed with busy life. "But, lo, how oftentimes misfortune doth search and pursue us, even then when we thinke to be at rest!" exclaims the unhappy Laudonnière. Amidst the light and cheer of reno-vated hope, a cloud of blackest omen was gathering in the east.

At half-past eleven on the night of Tuesday, the fourth of September, the crew of Ribaut's flag-ship, anchored on the still sea outside the bar, saw a huge hulk, grim with the throats of cannon, drifting towards them through the gloom; and from its stern rolled on the sluggish air the portentous banner of Spain.

CHAPTER VII.

1565.

MENENDEZ.

THE monk, the inquisitor, and the Jesuit were
lords of Spain, — sovereigns of her sovereign, for
they had formed the dark and narrow mind of that
tyrannical recluse. They had formed the minds of
her people, quenched in blood every spark of rising
heresy, and given over a noble nation to a bigotry
blind and inexorable as the doom of fate. Linked
with pride, ambition, avarice, every passion of a
rich, strong nature, potent for good and ill, it made
the Spaniard of that day a scourge as dire as ever fell
on man.

Day was breaking on the world. Light, hope, and
freedom pierced with vitalizing ray the clouds and

PEDRO MENENDEZ DE AVILÈS.

the miasma that hung so thick over the prostrate
Middle Age, once noble and mighty, now a foul
image of decay and death. Kindled with new life,
the nations gave birth to a progeny of heroes, and the
stormy glories of the sixteenth century rose on awak-
ened Europe. But Spain was the citadel of darkness, — a monastic cell, an inquisitorial dungeon,
where no ray could pierce. She was the bulwark of
the Church, against whose adamantine wall the waves
of innovation beat in vain.[1] In every country of
Europe the party of freedom and reform was the
national party, the party of reaction and absolutism
was the Spanish party, leaning on Spain, looking to
her for help. Above all, it was so in France; and,
while within her bounds there was for a time some
semblance of peace, the national and religious rage
burst forth on a wilder theatre. Thither it is for us
to follow it, where, on the shores of Florida, the
Spaniard and the Frenchman, the bigot and the
Huguenot, met in the grapple of death.

In a corridor of his palace, Philip the Second was
met by a man who had long stood waiting his
approach, and who with proud reverence placed a
petition in the hand of the pale and sombre King.

---

[1] "Better a ruined kingdom, true to itself and its king, than one left
unharmed to the profit of the Devil and the heretics." — *Correspon-
dance de Philippe II.*, cited by Prescott, *Philip II.*, Book III. c. 2,
note 36.

"A prince can do nothing more shameful, or more hurtful to himself, than to permit his people to live according to their conscience."
·— *The Duke of Alva*, in Davila, Lib. III. p. 341.

VOL. I. — 7

The petitioner was Pedro Menendez de Avilés, one of the ablest and most distinguished officers of the Spanish marine. He was born of an ancient Asturian family. His boyhood had been wayward, ungovernable, and fierce. He ran off at eight years of age, and when, after a search of six months, he was found and brought back, he ran off again. This time he was more successful, escaping on board a fleet bound against the Barbary corsairs, where his precocious appetite for blood and blows had reasonable contentment. A few years later, he found means to build a small vessel, in which he cruised against the corsairs and the French, and, though still hardly more than a boy, displayed a singular address and daring. The wonders of the New World now seized his imagination. He made a voyage thither, and the ships under his charge came back freighted with wealth. The war with France was then at its height. As captain-general of the fleet, he was sent with troops to Flanders; and to their prompt arrival was due, it is said, the victory of St. Quentin. Two years later, he commanded the luckless armada which bore back Philip to his native shore. On the way, the King narrowly escaped drowning in a storm off the port of Laredo. This mischance, or his own violence and insubordination, wrought to the prejudice of Menendez. He complained that his services were ill repaid. Philip lent him a favoring ear, and despatched him to the Indies as general of the fleet and army. Here he found means to amass vast riches; and, in

1561, on his return to Spain, charges were brought against him of a nature which his too friendly biographer does not explain. The Council of the Indies arrested him. He was imprisoned and sentenced to a heavy fine; but, gaining his release, hastened to court to throw himself on the royal clemency.[1] His petition was most graciously received. Philip restored his command, but remitted only half his fine, a strong presumption of his guilt.

Menendez kissed the royal hand; he had another petition in reserve. His son had been wrecked near the Bermudas, and he would fain go thither to find tidings of his fate. The pious King bade him trust in God, and promised that he should be despatched without delay to the Bermudas and to Florida, with a commission to make an exact survey of the neighboring seas for the profit of future voyagers; but Menendez was not content with such an errand. He knew, he said, nothing of greater moment to his Majesty than the conquest and settlement of Florida. The climate was healthful, the soil fertile; and, worldly advantages aside, it was peopled by a race sunk in the thickest shades of infidelity. "Such grief," he pursued, "seizes me, when I behold this multitude of wretched Indians, that I should choose the conquest and settling of Florida above all commands, offices, and dignities which your Majesty might bestow."[2] Those who take this for hypocrisy do not know the Spaniard of the sixteenth century.

[1] Barcia (Cardenas y Cano), *Ensayo Cronologico*, 57–64.
[2] *Ibid.*, 65.

The King was edified by his zeal. An enterprise
of such spiritual and temporal promise was not to be
slighted, and Menendez was empowered to conquer
and convert Florida at his own cost. The conquest
was to be effected within three years. Menendez was
to take with him five hundred men, and supply them
with five hundred slaves, besides horses, cattle, sheep,
and hogs. Villages were to be built, with forts to
defend them; and sixteen ecclesiastics, of whom four
should be Jesuits, were to form the nucleus of a Floridan church. The King, on his part, granted Menendez free trade with Hispaniola, Porto Rico, Cuba,
and Spain, the office of Adelantado of Florida for life,
with the right of naming his successor, and large emol-
uments to be drawn from the expected conquest.[1]

The compact struck, Menendez hastened to his
native Asturias to raise money among his relatives.
Scarcely was he gone, when tidings reached Madrid
that Florida was already occupied by a colony of
French Protestants, and that a reinforcement, under
Ribaut, was on the point of sailing thither. A
French historian of high authority declares that these
advices came from the Catholic party at the French
court, in whom every instinct of patriotism was lost
in their hatred of Coligny and the Huguenots. Of
this there can be little doubt, though information also
came about this time from the buccaneer Frenchmen
captured in the West Indies.

[1] The above is from Barcia, as the original compact has not been
found. For the patent conferring the title of "Adelantado," see
Coleccion de Varios Documentos, I. 13.

Foreigners had invaded the territory of Spain. The trespassers, too, were heretics, foes of God, and liegemen of the Devil. Their doom was fixed. But how would France endure an assault, in time of peace, on subjects who had gone forth on an enterprise sanctioned by the Crown, and undertaken in its name and under its commission?

The throne of France, in which the corruption of the nation seemed gathered to a head, was trembling between the two parties of the Catholics and the Huguenots, whose chiefs aimed at royalty. Flattering both, caressing both, playing one against the other, and betraying both, Catherine de Medicis, by a thousand crafty arts and expedients of the moment, sought to retain the crown on the head of her weak and vicious son. Of late her crooked policy had led her towards the Catholic party, in other words the party of Spain; and she had already given ear to the savage Duke of Alva, urging her to the course which, seven years later, led to the carnage of St. Bartholomew. In short, the Spanish policy was in the ascendant, and no thought of the national interest or honor could restrain that basest of courts from abandoning by hundreds to the national enemy those whom it was itself meditating to immolate by thousands.[1] It might protest for form's sake, or to quiet public

---

[1] The French Jesuit Charlevoix says: "On avoit donné à cette expédition tout l'air d'une guerre sainte, entreprise contre les Hérétiques de concert avec le Roy de France." Nor does Charlevoix seem to doubt this complicity of Charles the Ninth in an attack on his own subjects.

clamor; but Philip of Spain well knew that it would
end in patient submission.

Menendez was summoned back in haste to the
Spanish court. His force must be strengthened.
Three hundred and ninety-four men were added at
the royal charge, and a corresponding number of
transport and supply ships. It was a holy war, a
crusade, and as such was preached by priest and monk
along the western coasts of Spain. All the Biscayan
ports flamed with zeal, and adventurers crowded to
enroll themselves; since to plunder heretics is good
for the soul as well as the purse, and broil and massacre have double attraction when promoted into a
means of salvation. It was a fervor, deep and hot,
but not of celestial kindling; nor yet that buoyant
and inspiring zeal which, when the Middle Age was
in its youth and prime, glowed in the souls of Tancred,
Godfrey, and St. Louis, and which, when its day was
long since past, could still find its home in the great
heart of Columbus. A darker spirit urged the new
crusade, — born not of hope, but of fear, slavish in
its nature, the creature and the tool of despotism;
for the typical Spaniard of the sixteenth century was
not in strictness a fanatic, he was bigotry incarnate.

Heresy was a plague-spot, an ulcer to be eradicated
with fire and the knife, and this foul abomination
was infecting the shores which the Vicegerent of
Christ had given to the King of Spain, and which
the Most Catholic King had given to the Adelantado.
Thus would countless heathen tribes be doomed to an

eternity of flame, and the Prince of Darkness hold
his ancient sway unbroken; and for the Adelantado
himself, the vast outlays, the vast debts of his bold
Floridan venture would be all in vain, and his fortunes
be wrecked past redemption through these tools of
Satan. As a Catholic, as a Spaniard, and as an
adventurer, his course was clear.

The work assigned him was prodigious. He was
invested with power almost absolute, not merely over
the peninsula which now retains the name of Florida,
but over all North America, from Labrador to Mexico;
for this was the Florida of the old Spanish geographers,
and the Florida designated in the commission of
Menendez. It was a continent which he was to conquer and occupy out of his own purse. The impoverished King contracted with his daring and ambitious
subject to win and hold for him the territory of the
future United States and British Provinces. His
plan, as afterwards exposed at length in his letters to
Philip the Second, was, first, to plant a garrison at
Port Royal, and next to fortify strongly on Chesapeake Bay, called by him St. Mary's. He believed
that adjoining this bay was an arm of the sea, running northward and eastward, and communicating
with the Gulf of St. Lawrence, thus making New
England, with adjacent districts, an island. His
proposed fort on the Chesapeake, securing access, by
this imaginary passage, to the seas of Newfoundland,
would enable the Spaniards to command the fisheries,
on which both the French and the English had long

encroached, to the great prejudice of Spanish rights. Doubtless, too, these inland waters gave access to the South Sea, and their occupation was necessary to prevent the French from penetrating thither; for that ambitious people, since the time of Cartier, had never abandoned their schemes of seizing this portion of the dominions of the King of Spain. Five hundred soldiers and one hundred sailors must, he urges, take possession, without delay, of Port Royal and the Chesapeake.[1]

Preparation for his enterprise was pushed with furious energy. His whole force, when the several squadrons were united, amounted to two thousand six hundred and forty-six persons, in thirty-four vessels, one of which, the San Pelayo, bearing Menendez himself, was of nine hundred and ninety-six tons' burden, and is described as one of the finest ships afloat.[2] There were twelve Franciscans and eight Jesuits, besides other ecclesiastics; and many knights of Galicia, Biscay, and the Asturias took part in the

[1] *Cartas escritas al Rey por el General Pero Menendez de Avilés.* These are the official despatches of Menendez, of which the originals are preserved in the archives of Seville. They are very voluminous and minute in detail. Copies of them were obtained by the aid of Buckingham Smith, Esq., to whom the writer is also indebted for various other documents from the same source, throwing new light on the events described. Menendez calls Port Royal "St. Elena," a name afterwards applied to the sound which still retains it. Compare *Historical Magazine,* IV. 320.

[2] This was not so remarkable as it may appear. Charnock, *History of Marine Architecture,* gives the tonnage of the ships of the Invincible Armada. The flag-ship of the Andalusian squadron was of fifteen hundred and fifty tons; several were of about twelve hundred.

expedition. With a slight exception, the whole was at the Adelantado's charge. Within the first fourteen months, according to his admirer, Barcia, the adventure cost him a million ducats.[1]

Before the close of the year, Sancho de Arciniega was commissioned to join Menendez with an additional force of fifteen hundred men.[2]

Red-hot with a determined purpose, the Adelantado would brook no delay. To him, says the chronicler, every day seemed a year. He was eager to anticipate Ribaut, of whose designs and whose force he seems to have been informed to the minutest particular, but whom he hoped to thwart and ruin by gaining Fort Caroline before him. With eleven ships, therefore, he sailed from Cadiz, on the twenty-ninth of June, 1565, leaving the smaller vessels of his fleet to follow with what speed they might. He touched first at the Canaries, and on the eighth of July left them, steering for Dominica. A minute account of the voyage

[1] Barcia, 69. The following passage in one of the unpublished letters of Menendez seems to indicate that the above is exaggerated: "Your Majesty may be assured by me, that, had I a million, more or less, I would employ and spend the whole in this undertaking, it being so greatly to [the glory of] God our Lord, and the increase of our Holy Catholic Faith, and the service and authority of your Majesty; and thus I have offered to our Lord whatever He shall give me in this world, [and whatever] I shall possess, gain, or acquire shall be devoted to the planting of the Gospel in this land, and the enlightenment of the natives thereof, and this I do promise to your Majesty." This letter is dated 11 September, 1565.

[2] *Año de 1565. Nombramiento de Capitan-General de la Armada destinada para yr á la Provincia de la Florida al socorro del General Pero Menendez de Avilés, hecho por Su Magestad al Capitan Sancho de Arciniega.*

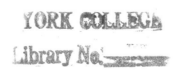

has come down to us, written by Mendoza, chaplain
of the expedition, — a somewhat dull and illiterate
person, who busily jots down the incidents of each
passing day, and is constantly betraying, with a certain awkward simplicity, how the cares of this world
and of the next jostle each other in his thoughts.

On Friday, the twentieth of July, a storm fell upon
them with appalling fury.   The pilots lost their wits,
and the sailors gave themselves up to their terrors.
Throughout the night, they beset Mendoza for confession and absolution, a boon not easily granted, for
the seas swept the crowded decks with cataracts of
foam, and the shriekings of the gale in the rigging
overpowered the exhortations of the half-drowned
priest.   Cannon, cables, spars, water-casks, were
thrown overboard, and the chests of the sailors would
have followed, had not the latter, in spite of their
fright, raised such a howl of remonstrance that the
order was revoked.   At length day dawned.   Plung-
ing, reeling, half under water, quivering with the
shock of the seas, whose mountain ridges rolled down
upon her before the gale, the ship lay in deadly peril
from Friday till Monday noon.   Then the storm
abated; the sun broke out; and again she held her
course.[1]

They reached Dominica on Sunday, the fifth of
August.   The chaplain tells us how he went on shore

[1] Francisco Lopez de Mendoza Grajales, *Relacion de la Jornada de
Pedro Menendez*, printed in *Coleccion de Documentos Inéditos*, III. 441
(Madrid, 1865).   There is a French translation in the *Floride* of
Ternaux-Compans.   Letter of Menendez to the King, 13 August, 1565.

to refresh himself; how, while his Italian servant washed his linen at a brook, he strolled along the beach and picked up shells; and how he was scared, first, by a prodigious turtle, and next by a vision of the cannibal natives, which caused his prompt retreat to the boats.

On the tenth, they anchored in the harbor of Porto Rico, where they found two ships of their squadron, from which they had parted in the storm. One of them was the "San Pelayo," with Menendez on board. Mendoza informs us, that in the evening the officers came on board the ship to which he was attached, when he, the chaplain, regaled them with sweetmeats, and that Menendez invited him not only to supper that night, but to dinner the next day, "for the which I thanked him, as reason was," says the gratified churchman.

Here thirty men deserted, and three priests also ran off, of which Mendoza bitterly complains, as increasing his own work. The motives of the clerical truants may perhaps be inferred from a worldly temptation to which the chaplain himself was subjected. "I was offered the service of a chapel where I should have got a *peso* for every mass I said, the whole year round; but I did not accept it, for fear that what I hear said of the other three would be said of me. Besides, it is not a place where one can hope for any great advancement, and I wished to try whether, in refusing a benefice for the love of the Lord, He will not repay me with some other stroke of fortune before the end of the voyage; for it is my aim to serve God and His blessed Mother." [1]

The original design had been to rendezvous at Havana, but with the Adelantado the advantages of despatch outweighed every other consideration. He resolved to push directly for Florida. Five of his scattered ships had by this time rejoined company, comprising, exclusive of officers, a force of about five hundred soldiers, two hundred sailors, and one hundred colonists. [2] Bearing northward, he advanced by an unknown and dangerous course along the coast of Hayti and through the intricate passes of the Bahamas. On the night of the twenty-sixth, the "San Pelayo" struck three times on the shoals; "but," says the chaplain, "inasmuch as our enterprise was undertaken for the sake of Christ and His blessed Mother, two heavy seas struck her abaft, and set her afloat again."

At length the ships lay becalmed in the Bahama Channel, slumbering on the glassy sea, torpid with the heats of a West Indian August. Menendez called a council of the commanders. There was doubt and indecision. Perhaps Ribaut had already reached the French fort, and then to attack the united force would be an act of desperation. Far better to await their lagging comrades. But the Adelantado was of another mind; and, even had his enemy arrived, he was resolved that he should have no time to fortify himself.

[1] Mendoza, *Relacion de la Jornada de Pedro Menendez.*
[2] Letter of Menendez to the King, 11 September, 1565.

"It is God's will," he said, "that our victory should be due, not to our numbers, but to His all-powerful aid. Therefore has He stricken us with tempests, and scattered our ships." [1] And he gave his voice for instant advance.

There was much dispute; even the chaplain remonstrated; but nothing could bend the iron will of Menendez. Nor was a sign of celestial approval wanting. At nine in the evening, a great meteor burst forth in mid-heaven, and, blazing like the sun, rolled westward towards the coast of Florida. [2] The fainting spirits of the crusaders were revived. Diligent preparation was begun. Prayers and masses were said; and, that the temporal arm might not fail, the men were daily practised on deck in shooting at marks, in order, says the chronicle, that the recruits might learn not to be afraid of their guns.

The dead calm continued. "We were all very tired," says the chaplain, "and I above all, with praying to God for a fair wind. To-day, at about two in the afternoon, He took pity on us, and sent us a breeze." [3] Before night they saw land, — the faint line of forest, traced along the watery horizon, that marked the coast of Florida. But where, in all this vast monotony, was the lurking-place of the French? Menendez anchored, and sent a captain with twenty men ashore, who presently found a band of Indians,

---

[1] Barcia, 70.

[2] Mendoza, *Relacion:* "Nos mostró Nuestro Señor un misterio en el cielo," etc.

[3] Mendoza, *Relacion.*

and gained from them the needed information. He stood northward, till, on the afternoon of Tuesday, the fourth of September, he descried four ships anchored near the mouth of a river. It was the river St. John's, and the ships were four of Ribaut's squadron. The prey was in sight. The Spaniards prepared for battle, and bore down upon the Lutherans; for, with them, all Protestants alike were branded with the name of the arch-heretic. Slowly, before the faint breeze, the ships glided on their way; but while, excited and impatient, the fierce crews watched the decreasing space, and when they were still three leagues from their prize, the air ceased to stir, the sails flapped against the mast, a black cloud with thunder rose above the coast, and the warm rain of the South descended on the breathless sea. It was dark before the wind stirred again and the ships resumed their course. At half-past eleven they reached the French. The "San Pelayo" slowly moved to windward of Ribaut's flag-ship, the "Trinity," and anchored very near her. The other ships took similar stations. While these preparations were making, a work of two hours, the men labored in silence, and the French, thronging their gangways, looked on in equal silence. "Never, since I came into the world," writes the chaplain, "did I know such a stillness."

It was broken at length by a trumpet from the deck of the "San Pelayo." A French trumpet answered. Then Menendez, "with much courtesy," says his

Spanish eulogist, inquired, "Gentlemen, whence does this fleet come?"

"From France," was the reply.

"What are you doing here?" pursued the Adelantado.

"Bringing soldiers and supplies for a fort which the King of France has in this country, and for many others which he soon will have."

"Are you Catholics or Lutherans?"

Many voices cried out together, "Lutherans, of the new religion." Then, in their turn, they demanded who Menendez was, and whence he came.

He answered: "I am Pedro Menendez, General of the fleet of the King of Spain, Don Philip the Second, who have come to this country to hang and behead all Lutherans whom I shall find by land or sea, according to instructions from my King, so precise that I have power to pardon none; and these commands I shall fulfil, as you will see. At daybreak I shall board your ships, and if I find there any Catholic, he shall be well treated; but every heretic shall die."[1]

[1] "Pedro Menendez os lo pregunta, General de esta Armada del Rei de España Don Felipe Segundo, qui viene à esta Tierra à ahorcar, y degollar todos los Luteranos, que hallare en ella, y en el Mar, segun la Instruccion, que trae de mi Rei, que es tan precisa, que me priva de la facultad de perdonarlos, y la cumplirè en todo, como lo vereis luego que amanezca, que entrarè en vuestros Navios, y si hallare algun Catolico, le harè buen tratamiento; pero el que fuere Herege, morirà." Barcia, 75.

The following is the version, literally given, of Menendez himself:

"I answered them: 'Pedro Menendez, who was going by your Majesty's command to this coast and country in order to burn and hang the Lutheran French who should be found there, and that in the

The French with one voice raised a cry of wrath and defiance.

"If you are a brave man, don't wait till day. Come on now, and see what you will get!"

And they assailed the Adelantado with a shower of scoffs and insults.

Menendez broke into a rage, and gave the order to board. The men slipped the cables, and the sullen black hulk of the "San Pelayo" drifted down upon the "Trinity." The French did not make good their defiance. Indeed, they were incapable of resistance, Ribaut with his soldiers being ashore at Fort Caroline. They cut their cables, left their anchors, made sail, and fled. The Spaniards fired, the French replied. The other Spanish ships had imitated the movement of the "San Pelayo;" "but," writes the chaplain, Mendoza, "these devils are such adroit sailors, and manœuvred so well, that we did not catch one of them."[1] Pursuers and pursued ran out to sea, firing useless volleys at each other.

morning I would board their ships to find out whether any of them belonged to that people, because, in case they did, I could not do otherwise than execute upon them that justice which your Majesty had ordained.'" Letter of Menendez to the King, 11 September, 1565.

[1] Mendoza, *Relacion.*

The above account is that of Barcia, the admirer and advocate of Menendez. A few points have been added from Mendoza, as indicated by the citations. One statement of Barcia is omitted, because there can be little doubt that it is false. He says, that, when the Spanish fleet approached, the French opened a heavy fire on them. Neither the fanatical Mendoza, who was present, nor the French writers, Laudonnière, Le Moyne, and Challeux, mention this circumstance, which, besides, can scarcely be reconciled with the subsequent conduct

In the morning Menendez gave over the chase, turned, and, with the "San Pelayo" alone, ran back for the St. John's.   But here a welcome was prepared for him.   He saw bands of armed men drawn up on the beach, and the smaller vessels of Ribaut's squadron, which had crossed the bar several days before, anchored behind it to oppose his landing.   He would not venture an attack, but, steering southward, sailed along the coast till he came to an inlet which he named San Agustin, the same which Laudonnière had named the River of Dolphins.

Here he found three of his ships already debarking their troops, guns, and stores.   Two officers, Patiño and Vicente, had taken possession of the dwelling of the Indian chief Seloy, a huge barn-like structure, strongly framed of entire trunks of trees, and thatched with palmetto leaves.[1]   Around it they were throwing up intrenchments of fascines and sand, and gangs of negroes were toiling at the work.   Such was the birth of St. Augustine, the oldest town of the United States.

On the eighth, Menendez took formal possession of his domain.   Cannon were fired, trumpets sounded,

of either party. Mendoza differs from Barcia also in respect to the time of the attack, which he places "at two hours after sunset." In other points his story tallies as nearly as could be expected with that of Barcia. The same may be said of Challeux and Laudonnière. The latter says, that the Spaniards, before attacking, asked after the French officers by name, whence he infers that they had received very minute information from France.

[1] Compare Hawkins, *Second Voyage*. He visited this or some similar structure, and his journalist minutely describes it.

VOL. I. — 8

and banners displayed, as he landed in state at the head of his officers and nobles. Mendoza, crucifix in hand, came to meet him, chanting *Te Deum laudamus,* while the Adelantado and all his company, kneeling, kissed the crucifix, and the assembled Indians gazed in silent wonder.[1]

Meanwhile the tenants of Fort Caroline were not idle. Two or three soldiers, strolling along the beach in the afternoon, had first seen the Spanish ships, and hastily summoned Ribaut. He came down to the mouth of the river, followed by an anxious and excited crowd; but, as they strained their eyes through the darkness, they could see nothing but the flashes of the distant guns. At length the returning light showed, far out at sea, the Adelantado in hot chase of their flying comrades. Pursuers and pursued were soon out of sight. The drums beat to arms. After many hours of suspense, the "San Pelayo" reappeared, hovering about the mouth of the river, then bearing away towards the south. More anxious hours ensued, when three other sail came in sight, and they recognized three of their own returning ships. Communication was opened, a boat's crew landed, and they learned from Cosette, one of the French captains, that, confiding in the speed of his ship, he had followed the Spaniards to St. Augustine, reconnoitred their position, and seen them land their negroes and intrench themselves.[2]

[1] Mendoza, *Relacion.*
[2] Laudonnière in Basanier, 105. Le Moyne differs in a few trifling details.

Laudonnière lay sick in bed in his chamber at Fort Caroline when Ribaut entered, and with him La Grange, Sainte Marie, Ottigny, Yonville, and other officers. At the bedside of the displaced command ant, they held their council of war. Three plans were proposed: first, to remain where they were and fortify themselves; next, to push overland for St. Augustine and attack the invaders in their intrench- ments; and, finally, to embark and assail them by sea. The first plan would leave their ships a prey to the Spaniards; and so, too, in all likelihood, would the second, besides the uncertainties of an overland march through an unknown wilderness. By sea, the distance was short and the route explored. By a sudden blow they could capture or destroy the Spanish ships, and master the troops on shore before reinforce- ments could arrive, and before they had time to com- plete their defences.[1]

Such were the views of Ribaut, with which, not unnaturally, Laudonnière finds fault, and Le Moyne echoes the censures of his chief. And yet the plan seems as well conceived as it was bold, lacking noth- ing but success. The Spaniards, stricken with terror, owed their safety to the elements, or, as they say,

---

[1] Ribaut showed Laudonnière a letter from Coligny, appended to which were these words: "Captaine *Jean Ribaut:* En fermant ceste lettre i'ay eu certain aduis, comme dom *Petro Melandes* se part d'Espagne, pour aller à la coste de la Nouvelle Fráce: Vous regarderez de n'endurer qu'il n'entrepreine sur nous, non plus qu'il veut que nous n'entreprenions sur eux." Ribaut interpreted this into a command to attack the Spaniards. Laudonnière, 106.

to the special interposition of the Holy Virgin.
Menendez was a leader fit to stand with Cortés and
Pizarro; but he was matched with a man as cool,
skilful, prompt, and daring as himself. The traces
that have come down to us indicate in Ribaut one far
above the common stamp, — "a distinguished man, of
many high qualities," as even the fault-finding Le
Moyne calls him; devout after the best spirit of the
Reform; and with a human heart under his steel
breastplate.

La Grange and other officers took part with Laudonnière, and opposed the plan of an attack by sea;
but Ribaut's conviction was unshaken, and the order
was given.   All his own soldiers fit for duty embarked
in haste, and with them went La Caille, Arlac, and,
as it seems, Ottigny, with the best of Laudonnière's
men.   Even Le Moyne, though wounded in the fight
with Outina's warriors, went on board to bear his part
in the fray, and would have sailed with the rest had
not Ottigny, seeing his disabled condition, ordered him
back to the fort.

On the tenth, the ships, crowded with troops, set
sail.   Ribaut was gone, and with him the bone and
sinew of the colony.   The miserable remnant watched
his receding sails with dreary foreboding, — a foreboding which seemed but too just, when, on the next
day, a storm, more violent than the Indians had ever
known,[1] howled through the forest and lashed the
ocean into fury.   Most forlorn was the plight of these

[1] Laudonnière, 107.

exiles, left, it might be, the prey of a band of ferocious bigots more terrible than the fiercest hordes of
the wilderness; and when night closed on the stormy
river and the gloomy waste of pines, what dreams of
terror may not have haunted the helpless women who
crouched under the hovels of Fort Caroline!

The fort was in a ruinous state, with the palisade
on the water side broken down, and three breaches in
the rampart.   In the driving rain, urged by the sick
Laudonnière, the men, bedrenched and disheartened,
labored as they could to strengthen their defences.
Their muster-roll shows but a beggarly array.   "Now,"
says Laudonnière, "let them which have bene bold to
say that I had men ynough left me, so that I had
meanes to defend my selfe, give eare a little now vnto
mee, and if they have eyes in their heads, let them
see what men I had."   Of Ribaut's followers left at
the fort, only nine or ten had weapons, while only
two or three knew how to use them.   Four of them
were boys, who kept Ribaut's dogs, and another was
his cook.   Besides these, he had left a brewer, an old
crossbow-maker, two shoemakers, a player on the
spinet, four valets, a carpenter of threescore, —
Challeux, no doubt, who has left us the story of his
woes, — with a crowd of women, children, and eighty-
six camp-followers.[1]   To these were added the remnant of Laudonnière's men, of whom seventeen could
bear arms, the rest being sick or disabled by wounds
received in the fight with Outina.

---

[1] The muster-roll is from Laudonnière. Hakluyt's translation is
incorrect.

Laudonnière divided his force, such as it was, into two watches, over which he placed two officers, Saint Cler and La Vigne, gave them lanterns for going the rounds, and an hour-glass for setting the time; while he himself, giddy with weakness and fever, was every night at the guard-room.

It was the night of the nineteenth of September, the season of tempests; floods of rain drenched the sentries on the rampart, and, as day dawned on the dripping barracks and deluged parade, the storm increased in violence. What enemy could venture out on such a night? La Vigne, who had the watch, took pity on the sentries and on himself, dismissed them, and went to his quarters. He little knew what human energies, urged by ambition, avarice, bigotry, and desperation, will dare and do.

To return to the Spaniards at St. Augustine. On the morning of the eleventh, the crew of one of their smaller vessels, lying outside the bar, with Menendez himself on board, saw through the tw·light of early dawn two of Ribaut's ships close upon them. Not a breath of air was stirring. There was no escape, and the Spaniards fell on their knees in supplication to Our Lady of Utrera, explaining to her that the heretics were upon them, and begging her to send them a little wind. "Forthwith," says Mendoza, "one would have said that Our Lady herself came down upon the vessel." [1] A wind sprang up, and the Spaniards

---

[1] Mendoza, *Relacion*. Menendez, too, imputes the escape to divine interposition. "Our Lord permitted by a miracle that we should be saved." Letter of Menendez to the King, 15 October, 1565.

found refuge behind the bar. The returning day showed to their astonished eyes all the ships of Ribaut, their decks black with men, hovering off the entrance of the port; but Heaven had them in its charge, and again they experienced its protecting care. The breeze sent by Our Lady of Utrera rose to a gale, then to a furious tempest; and the grateful Adelantado saw through rack and mist the ships of his enemy tossed wildly among the raging waters as they struggled to gain an offing. With exultation in his heart, the skilful seaman read their danger, and saw them in his mind's eye dashed to utter wreck among the sand-bars and breakers of the lee shore.

A bold thought seized him. He would march overland with five hundred men, and attack Fort Caroline while its defenders were absent. First he ordered a mass, and then he called a council. Doubtless it was in that great Indian lodge of Seloy, where he had made his headquarters; and here, in this dim and smoky abode, nobles, officers, and priests gathered at his summons. There were fears and doubts and murmurings, but Menendez was desperate; not with the mad desperation that strikes wildly and at random, but the still white heat that melts and burns and seethes with a steady, unquenchable fierceness. "Comrades," he said, "the time has come to show our courage and our zeal. This is God's war, and we must not flinch. It is a war with Lutherans, and we must wage it with blood and fire." [1]

---

[1] "A sangre y fuego." Barcia, 78, where the speech is given at length.

But his hearers gave no response. They had not a million of ducats at stake, and were not ready for a cast so desperate. A clamor of remonstrance rose from the circle. Many voices, that of Mendoza among the rest, urged waiting till their main forces should arrive. The excitement spread to the men without, and the swarthy, black-bearded crowd broke into tumults mounting almost to mutiny, while an officer was heard to say that he would not go on such a hare-brained errand to be butchered like a beast. But nothing could move the Adelantado. His appeals or his threats did their work at last; the confusion was quelled, and preparation was made for the march.

On the morning of the seventeenth, five hundred arquebusiers and pikemen were drawn up before the camp. To each was given six pounds of biscuit and a canteen filled with wine. Two Indians and a rene-gade Frenchman, called François Jean, were to guide them, and twenty Biscayan axemen moved to the front to clear the way. Through floods of driving rain, a hoarse voice shouted the word of command, and the sullen march began.

With dismal misgiving, Mendoza watched the last files as they vanished in the tempestuous forest. Two days of suspense ensued, when a messenger came back with a letter from the Adelantado, announcing that he had nearly reached the French fort, and that on the morrow, September the twentieth, at sunrise, he hoped to assault it. "May the Divine Majesty deign

to protect us, for He knows that we have need of it,"
writes the scared chaplain; "the Adelantado's great
zeal and courage make us hope he will succeed, but,
for the good of his Majesty's service, he ought to be
a little less ardent in pursuing his schemes."

Meanwhile the five hundred pushed their march,
now toiling across the inundated savannas, waist-deep
in bulrushes and mud; now filing through the open
forest to the moan and roar of the storm-racked pines;
now hacking their way through palmetto thickets;
and now turning from their path to shun some pool,
quagmire, cypress swamp, or "hummock," matted
with impenetrable bushes, brambles, and vines.   As
they bent before the tempest, the water trickling from
the rusty head-piece crept clammy and cold betwixt
the armor and the skin; and when they made their
wretched bivouac, their bed was the spongy soil, and
the exhaustless clouds their tent.[1]

The night of Wednesday, the nineteenth, found
their vanguard in a deep forest of pines, less than a
mile from Fort Caroline, and near the low hills which
extended in its rear, and formed a continuation of St.
John's Bluff.   All around was one great morass.   In
pitchy darkness, knee-deep in weeds and water, half
starved, worn with toil and lack of sleep, drenched to
the skin, their provisions spoiled, their ammunition
wet, and their spirit chilled out of them, they stood
in shivering groups, cursing the enterprise and the

---

[1] I have examined the country on the line of march of Menendez.
In many places it retains its original features.

author of it. Menendez heard Fernando Perez, an
ensign, say aloud to his comrades: "This Asturian
Corito, who knows no more of war on shore than an
ass, has betrayed us all. By God, if my advice had
been followed, he would have had his deserts, the
day he set out on this cursed journey!"[1]

The Adelantado pretended not to hear.

Two hours before dawn he called his officers about
him. All night, he said, he had been praying to
God and the Virgin.

"Señores, what shall we resolve on? Our ammunition and provisions are gone. Our case is desperate."[2] And he urged a bold rush on the fort.

But men and officers alike were disheartened and
disgusted. They listened coldly and sullenly; many
were for returning at every risk; none were in the
mood for fight. Menendez put forth all his eloquence,
till at length the dashed spirits of his followers were
so far revived that they consented to follow him.

All fell on their knees in the marsh; then, rising,
they formed their ranks and began to advance, guided
by the renegade Frenchman, whose hands, to make
sure of him, were tied behind his back. Groping
and stumbling in the dark among trees, roots, and
underbrush, buffeted by wind and rain, and lashed in

[1] "Como nos trae vendidos este Asturiano Corito, que no sabe de
Guerra de Tierra, mas que un Jumento!" etc. Barcia, 79. *Corito* is a
nickname given to the inhabitants of Biscay and the Asturias.

[2] "Ved aora, Señores, què determinacion tomarèmos, hallandonos
cansados, perdidos, sin Municiones ni Comida, ni esperança de remedi-
arnos?" Barcia, 79.

the face by the recoiling boughs which they could not see, they soon lost their way, fell into confusion, and came to a stand, in a mood more savagely desponding than before.   But soon a glimmer of returning day came to their aid, and showed them the dusky sky, and the dark columns of the surrounding pines. Menendez ordered the men forward on pain of death. They obeyed, and presently, emerging from the forest, could dimly discern the ridge of a low hill, behind which, the Frenchman told them, was the fort. Menendez, with a few officers and men, cautiously mounted to the top.   Beneath lay Fort Caroline, three bow-shots distant; but the rain, the imperfect light, and a cluster of intervening houses prevented his seeing clearly, and he sent two officers to reconnoitre.   As they descended, they met a solitary Frenchman.   They knocked him down with a sheathed sword, wounded him, took him prisoner, kept him for a time, and then stabbed him as they returned towards the top of the hill.   Here, clutching their weapons, all the gang stood in fierce expectancy.

"Santiago!" cried Menendez.   "At them! God is with us!   Victory!"[1]   And, shouting their hoarse war-cries, the Spaniards rushed down the slope like starved wolves.

Not a sentry was on the rampart.   La Vigne, the officer of the guard, had just gone to his quarters; but a trumpeter, who chanced to remain, saw, through sheets of rain, the swarm of assailants sweeping down

[1] Barcia, 80.

the hill.   He blew the alarm, and at the summons a
few half-naked soldiers ran wildly out of the barracks.
It was too late.   Through the breaches and over the
ramparts the Spaniards came pouring in, with shouts
of "Santiago! Santiago!"

Sick men leaped from their beds.   Women and
children, blind with fright, darted shrieking from the
houses.   A fierce, gaunt visage, the thrust of a pike,
or blow of a rusty halberd, — such was the greeting
that met all alike.   Laudonnière snatched his sword
and target, and ran towards the principal breach, calling to his soldiers.   A rush of Spaniards met him;
his men were cut down around him; and he, with a
soldier named Bartholomew, was forced back into the
yard of his house.   Here stood a tent, and, as the
pursuers stumbled among the cords, he escaped behind
Ottigny's house, sprang through the breach in the
western rampart, and fled for the woods.[1]

Le Moyne had been one of the guard.   Scarcely
had he thrown himself into a hammock which was
slung in his room, when a savage shout, and a wild
uproar of shrieks, outcries, and the clash of weapons,
brought him to his feet.   He rushed by two Spaniards
in the doorway, ran behind the guard-house, leaped
through an embrasure into the ditch, and escaped to
the forest.[2]

Challeux, the carpenter, was going betimes to his
work, a chisel in his hand.   He was old, but pike and
partisan brandished at his back gave wings to his

---

[1] Laudonnière, 110; Le Moyne, 24.   [2] Le Moyne, 25.

flight.   In the ecstasy of his terror, he leaped upward, clutched the top of the palisade, and threw himself over with the agility of a boy.   He ran up the hill, no one pursuing, and, as he neared the edge of the forest, turned and looked back.   From the high ground where he stood, he could see the butchery, the fury of the conquerors, and the agonizing gestures of the victims.   He turned again in horror, and plunged into the woods.[1]   As he tore his way through the briers and thickets, he met several fugitives escaped like himself.   Others presently came up, haggard and wild, like men broken loose from the jaws of death.   They gathered together and consulted.   One of them, known as Master Robert, in great repute for his knowledge of the Bible, was for returning and surrendering to the Spaniards.   "They are men," he said; "perhaps, when their fury is over, they will spare our lives; and, even if they kill us, it will only be a few moments' pain.   Better so, than to starve here in the woods, or be torn to pieces by wild beasts."[2]

The greater part of the naked and despairing company assented, but Challeux was of a different mind. The old Huguenot quoted Scripture, and called the names of prophets and apostles to witness, that, in the direst extremity, God would not abandon those who rested their faith in Him.   Six of the fugitives, however, still held to their desperate purpose.   Issuing from the woods, they descended towards the fort,

[1] Challeux in Ternaux-Compans, 272.   [2] Ibid., 275.

and, as with beating hearts their comrades watched
the result, a troop of Spaniards rushed out, hewed
them down with swords and halberds, and dragged
their bodies to the brink of the river, where the
victims of the massacre were already flung in heaps.

Le Moyne, with a soldier named Grandchemin,
whom he had met in his flight, toiled all day through
the woods and marshes, in the hope of reaching the
small vessels anchored behind the bar. Night found
them in a morass. No vessel could be seen, and the
soldier, in despair, broke into angry upbraidings
against his companion, — saying that he would go
back and give himself up. Le Moyne at first opposed
him, then yielded. But when they drew near the
fort, and heard the uproar of savage revelry that
rose from within, the artist's heart failed him. He
embraced his companion, and the soldier advanced
alone. A party of Spaniards came out to meet him.
He kneeled, and begged for his life. He was answered
by a death-blow; and the horrified Le Moyne, from
his hiding-place in the thicket, saw his limbs hacked
apart, stuck on pikes, and borne off in triumph.[1]

Meanwhile, Menendez, mustering his followers, had
offered thanks to God for their victory; and this
pious butcher wept with emotion as he recounted the
favors which Heaven had showered upon their enterprise. His admiring historian gives it in proof of his
humanity, that, after the rage of the assault was
spent, he ordered that women, infants, and boys under

[1] Le Moyne, 26.

fifteen should thenceforth be spared. Of these, by
his own account, there were about fifty. Writing in
October to the King, he says that they cause him
great anxiety, since he fears the anger of God should
he now put them to death in cold blood, while, on
the other hand, he is in dread lest the venom of their
heresy should infect his men.

A hundred and forty-two persons were slain in and
around the fort, and their bodies lay heaped together
on the bank of the river. Nearly opposite was
anchored a small vessel, called the "Pearl," commanded by Jacques Ribaut, son of the Admiral. The
ferocious soldiery, maddened with victory and drunk
with blood, crowded to the water's edge, shouting
insults to those on board, mangling the corpses, tear-
ing out their eyes, and throwing them towards the
vessel from the points of their daggers.[1] Thus did
the Most Catholic Philip champion the cause of
Heaven in the New World.

It was currently believed in France, and, though
no eye-witness attests it, there is reason to think it
true, that among those murdered at Fort Caroline
there were some who died a death of peculiar ignominy. Menendez, it is affirmed, hanged his prisoners

---

[1] " . . . car, arrachans les yeux des morts, les fichoyent au bout des
dagues, et puis auec cris, heurlemens & toute gaudisserie, les iettoyent
contre nos François vers l'eau." Challeux (1566), 34.

" Ils arrachèrent les yeulx qu'ils avoient meurtris, et les aiant fichez
à la poincte de leurs dagues faisoient entre eulx à qui plus loing les
jetteroit." Prévost, *Reprinse de la Floride*. This is a contemporary
MS. in the Bibliothèque Nationale, printed by Ternaux-Compans in his
Recueil. It will be often cited hereafter.

on trees, and placed over them the inscription, "I do this, not as to Frenchmen, but as to Lutherans."[1]

The Spaniards gained a great booty in armor, clothing, and provisions. "Nevertheless," says the devout Mendoza, after closing his inventory of the plunder, "the greatest profit of this victory is the triumph which our Lord has granted us, whereby His holy Gospel will be introduced into this country, a thing so needful for saving so many souls from perdition." Again he writes in his journal, "We owe to God and His Mother, more than to human strength, this victory over the adversaries of the holy Catholic religion."

To whatever influence, celestial or other, the exploit may best be ascribed, the victors were not yet quite content with their success. Two small French vessels, besides that of Jacques Ribaut, still lay within range of the fort. When the storm had a little abated, the cannon were turned on them. One of them was sunk, but Ribaut, with the others, escaped down the river, at the mouth of which several light craft, including that bought from the English, had been anchored since the arrival of his father's squadron.

While this was passing, the wretched fugitives were flying from the scene of massacre through a tempest, of whose persistent violence all the narratives speak with wonder. Exhausted, starved, half

[1] Prévost in Ternaux-Compans, 357; Lescarbot (1612), I. 127; Charlevoix, *Nouvelle France* (1744), I. 81; and nearly all the French secondary writers. Barcia denies the story. How deep the indignation it kindled in France will appear hereafter.

naked, ·— for most of them had escaped in their shirts,
— they pushed their toilsome way amid the ceaseless
wrath of the elements. A few sought refuge in
Indian villages; but these, it is said, were afterwards
killed by the Spaniards. The greater number attempted to reach the vessels at the mouth of the
river. Among the latter was Le Moyne, who, not-
withstanding his former failure, was toiling through
the mazes of tangled forests, when he met a Belgian
soldier, with the woman described as Laudonnière's
maid-servant, who was wounded in the breast; and,
urging their flight towards the vessels, they fell in
with other fugitives, including Laudonnière himself.
As they struggled through the salt marsh, the rank
sedge cut their naked limbs, and the tide rose to their
waists. Presently they descried others, toiling like
themselves through the matted vegetation, and recognized Challeux and his companions, also in quest of
the vessels. The old man still, as he tells us, held
fast to his chisel, which had done good service in
cutting poles to aid the party to cross the deep
creeks that channelled the morass. The united band,
twenty-six in all, were cheered at length by the sight
of a moving sail. It was the vessel of Captain
Mallard, who, informed of the massacre, was standing along shore in the hope of picking up some of the
fugitives. He saw their signals, and sent boats to
their rescue; but such was their exhaustion, that,
had not the sailors, wading to their armpits among
the rushes, borne them out on their shoulders, few

could have escaped.   Laudonnière was so feeble that
nothing but the support of a soldier, who held him
upright in his arms, had saved him from drowning
in the marsh.

On gaining the friendly decks, the fugitives counselled together.   One and all, they sickened for the
sight of France.

After waiting a few days, and saving a few more
stragglers from the marsh, they prepared to sail.
Young Ribaut, though ignorant of his father's fate,
assented with something more than willingness;
indeed, his behavior throughout had been stamped
with weakness and poltroonery.   On the twenty-fifth
of September they put to sea in two vessels; and,
after a voyage the privations of which were fatal to
many of them, they arrived, one party at Rochelle,
the other at Swansea, in Wales.

CHAPTER VIII.

1565.

MASSACRE OF THE HERETICS.

MENENDEZ RETURNS TO ST. AUGUSTINE. — TIDINGS OF THE FRENCH.
— RIBAUT SHIPWRECKED. — THE MARCH OF MENENDEZ. — HE
DISCOVERS THE FRENCH. — INTERVIEWS. — HOPES OF MERCY.
— SURRENDER OF THE FRENCH. — MASSACRE. — RETURN TO ST.
AUGUSTINE. — TIDINGS OF RIBAUT'S PARTY. — HIS INTERVIEW
WITH MENENDEZ. — DECEIVED AND BETRAYED. — MURDERED. —
ANOTHER MASSACRE. — FRENCH ACCOUNTS. — SCHEMES OF THE
SPANIARDS. — SURVIVORS OF THE CARNAGE.

IN suspense and fear, hourly looking seaward for
the dreaded fleet of Jean Ribaut, the chaplain Mendoza
and his brother priests held watch and ward at St.
Augustine in the Adelantado's absence. Besides
the celestial guardians whom they ceased not to
invoke, they had as protectors Bartholomew Menendez, the brother of the Adelantado, and about a hundred soldiers. Day and night they toiled to throw
up earthworks and strengthen their position.

A week elapsed, when they saw a man running
towards them, shouting as he ran.

Mendoza went to meet him.

"Victory! victory!" gasped the breathless messenger. "The French fort is ours!" .And he flung
his arms about the chaplain's neck.[1]

[1] Mendoza, *Relacion.*

"To-day," writes the priest in his journal, "Monday, the twenty-fourth, came our good general himself, with fifty soldiers, very tired, like all those who were with him. As soon as they told me he was coming, I ran to my lodging, took a new cassock, the best I had, put on my surplice, and went out to meet him with a crucifix in my hand; whereupon he, like a gentleman and a good Christian, kneeled down with all his followers, and gave the Lord a thousand thanks for the great favors he had received from Him."

In solemn procession, with four priests in front chanting *Te Deum*, the victors entered St. Augustine in triumph.

On the twenty-eighth, when the weary Adelantado was taking his siesta under the sylvan roof of Seloy, a troop of Indians came in with news that quickly roused him from his slumbers. They had seen a French vessel wrecked on the coast towards the south. Those who escaped from her were four or six leagues off, on the banks of a river or arm of the sea, which they could not cross.[1]

Menendez instantly sent forty or fifty men in boats to reconnoitre. Next, he called the chaplain, — for he would fain have him at his elbow to countenance the deeds he meditated, — and, with him twelve soldiers and two Indian guides, embarked in another boat. They rowed along the channel between Anas-

---

[1] Mendoza, *Relacion;* Solís in Barcia, 85; Letter of Menendez to the King, 18 October, 1565.

tasia Island and the main shore; then they landed, struck across the island on foot, traversed plains and marshes, reached the sea towards night, and searched along shore till ten o'clock to find their comrades who had gone before.   At length, with mutual joy, the two parties met, and bivouacked together on the sands.   Not far distant they could see lights.   These were the camp-fires of the shipwrecked French.

To relate with precision the fortunes of these un-happy men is impossible; for henceforward the French narratives are no longer the narratives of eye-wit-nesses.

It has been seen how, when on the point of assail-ing the Spaniards at St. Augustine, Jean Ribaut was thwarted by a gale, which they hailed as a divine interposition.   The gale rose to a tempest of strange fury.   Within a few days, all the French ships were cast on shore, between Matanzas Inlet and Cape Canaveral.   According to a letter of Menendez, many of those on board were lost; but others affirm that all escaped but a captain, La Grange, an officer of high merit, who was washed from a floating mast.[1]   One of the ships was wrecked at a point farther northward than the rest, and it was her company whose camp-fires were seen by the Spaniards at their bivouac on the sands of Anastasia Island.   They were endeavor-ing to reach Fort Caroline, of the fate of which they knew nothing, while Ribaut with the remainder was

[1] Challeux (1566), 46.

farther southward, struggling through the wilderness towards the same goal. What befell the latter will appear hereafter. Of the fate of the former party there is no French record. What we know of it is due to three Spanish eye-witnesses, Mendoza, Doctor Solís de las Meras, and Menendez himself. Solís was a priest, and brother-in-law to Menendez. Like Mendoza, he minutely describes what he saw, and, like him, was a red-hot zealot, lavishing applause on the darkest deeds of his chief. But the principal witness, though not the most minute or most trustworthy, is Menendez, in his long despatches sent from Florida to the King, and now first brought to light from the archives of Seville, — a cool record of unsurpassed atrocities, inscribed on the back with the royal indorsement, "Say to him that he has done well."

When the Adelantado saw the French fires in the distance, he lay close in his bivouac, and sent two soldiers to reconnoitre. At two o'clock in the morning they came back, and reported that it was impossible to get at the enemy, since they were on the farther side of an arm of the sea (Matanzas Inlet). Menendez, however, gave orders to march, and before daybreak reached the hither bank, where he hid his men in a bushy hollow. Thence, as it grew light, they could discern the enemy, many of whom were searching along the sands and shallows for shell-fish, for they were famishing. A thought struck Menendez, an inspiration, says Mendoza, of the Holy

NIHIL OMNI EX PAR-
TE BEATVM .

RÉNÉ DE LAUDONNIÈRE.

Spirit.[1] He put on the clothes of a sailor, entered a boat which had been brought to the spot, and rowed towards the shipwrecked men, the better to learn their condition. A Frenchman swam out to meet him. Menendez demanded what men they were.

"Followers of Ribaut, Viceroy of the King of France," answered the swimmer.

"Are you Catholics or Lutherans?"

"All Lutherans."

A brief dialogue ensued, during which the Adelantado declared his name and character, and the Frenchman gave an account of the designs of Ribaut, and of the disaster that had thwarted them.   He then swam back to his companions, but soon returned, and asked safe conduct for his captain and four other gentlemen, who wished to hold conference with the Spanish general. Menendez gave his word for their safety, and, returning to the shore, sent his boat to bring them over. On their landing, he met them very courteously.   His followers were kept at a distance, so disposed behind hills and among bushes as to give an exaggerated idea of their force, — a precaution the more needful, as they were only about sixty in number, while the French, says Solís, were above two hundred. Menendez, however, declares that they did not exceed a hundred and forty. The French officer told him the story of their shipwreck, and begged him to lend them a boat to aid them in cross-

---

[1] " Nuestro buen General, alumbrado por el Espíritu Santo, dixo," etc.

ing the rivers which lay between them and a fort of their King, whither they were making their way.

Then came again the ominous question, —

"Are you Catholics or Lutherans?"

"We are Lutherans."

"Gentlemen," pursued Menendez, "your fort is taken, and all in it are put to the sword." And, in proof of his declaration, he caused articles plundered from Fort Caroline to be shown to the unhappy petitioners. He then left them, and went to breakfast with his officers, first ordering food to be placed before them. Having breakfasted, he returned to them.

"Are you convinced now," he asked, "that what I have told you is true?"

The French captain assented, and implored him to lend them ships in which to return home. Menendez answered that he would do so willingly if they were Catholics, and if he had ships to spare, but he had none. The supplicants then expressed the hope that at least they and their followers would be allowed to remain with the Spaniards till ships could be sent to their relief, since there was peace between the two nations, whose kings were friends and brothers.

"All Catholics," retorted the Spaniard, "I will befriend; but as you are of the New Sect, I hold you as enemies, and wage deadly war against you; and this I will do with all cruelty [*crueldad*] in this country, where I command as Viceroy and Captain-General for my King. I am here to plant the Holy

Gospel, that the Indians may be enlightened and come to the knowledge of the Holy Catholic faith of our Lord Jesus Christ, as the Roman Church teaches it. If you will give up your arms and banners, and place yourselves at my mercy, you may do so, and I will act towards you as God shall give me grace. Do as you will, for other than this you can have neither truce nor friendship with me."[1]

Such were the Adelantado's words, as reported by a bystander, his admiring brother-in-law; and that they contain an implied assurance of mercy has been held, not only by Protestants, but by Catholics and Spaniards.[2] The report of Menendez himself is more brief, and sufficiently equivocal: —

"I answered, that they could give up their arms and place themselves under my mercy, — that I should do with them what our Lord should order; and from that I did not depart, nor would I, unless God our Lord should otherwise inspire."[3]

---

[1] " . . . mas, que por ser ellos de la Nueva Secta, los tenia por Enemigos, è tenia con ellos Guerra, à sangre, è fuego; è que esta la haria con toda crueldad à los que hallase en aquella Mar, è Tierra, donde era Virrei, è Capitan General por su Rei; è que iba à plantar el Santo Evangelio en aquella Tierra, para que fuesen alumbrados los Indios, è viniesen al conocimiento de la Santa Fè Catolica de Jesu Christo N. S. como lo dice, è canta la Iglesia Romana; è que si ellos quieren entregarle las Vanderas, è las Armas, è ponerse en su Misericordia, lo pueden hacer, para que èl haga de ellos lo que Dios le diere de gracia, ò que hogan lo que quisieren, que otras Treguas, ni Amistades no avian de hacer con èl." Solís, 86.

[2] Salazar, *Crisis del Ensayo*, 23; Padre Felipe Briet, *Anales.*

[3] " Respondíles, que las armas me podia rendir y ponerse debaxo de mi gracia para que Yo hiciese dellos aquello que Nuestro Señor me

One of the Frenchmen recrossed to consult with
his companions. In two hours he returned, and
offered fifty thousand ducats to secure their lives;
but Menendez, says his brother-in-law, would give
no pledges. On the other hand, expressions in his
own despatches point to the inference that a virtual
pledge was given, at least to certain individuals.

The starving French saw no resource but to yield
themselves to his mercy. The boat was again sent
across the river. It returned laden with banners,
arquebuses, swords, targets, and helmets. The
Adelantado ordered twenty soldiers to bring over the
prisoners, ten at a time. He then took the French
officers aside behind a ridge of sand, two gunshots
from the bank. Here, with courtesy on his lips and
murder at his heart, he said: —

"Gentlemen, I have but few men, and you are so
many that, if you were free, it would be easy for you
to take your satisfaction on us for the people we
killed when we took your fort. Therefore it is
necessary that you should go to my camp, four
leagues from this place, with your hands tied."[1]

ordenase, y de aquí no me sacó, ní sacára si Dios Nuestro Señor no
espiára en mi otra cosa. Y ansi se fué con esta respuesta, y se vinieron
y me entregaron las armas, y hiceles amarrar las manos atras y
pasarlos à cuchillo. . . . Parecióme que castigarlos desta manera se
servia Dios Nuestro Señor, y V. Mag^d, para que adelante nos dexen
mas libres esta mala seta para plantar el evangelio en estas partes." —
Carta de Pedro Menendez á su Magestad, Fuerte de S^n Agustin, 15
Octubre, 1565.

[1] "Señores, yo tengo poca Gente, è no mui conocida, è Vosotros sois
muchos è andando sueltos, facil cosa os seria satisfaceros de Nosotros,

Accordingly, as each party landed, they were led
out of sight behind the sand-hill, and their hands tied
behind their backs with the match-cords of the arquebuses, though not before each had been supplied with
food.   The whole day passed before all were brought
together, bound and helpless, under the eye of the
inexorable Adelantado.   But now Mendoza inter-
posed. "I was a priest," he says, "and had the
bowels of a man." He asked that if there were
Christians — that is to say, Catholics — among the
prisoners, they should be set apart.   Twelve Breton
sailors professed themselves to be such; and these,
together with four carpenters and calkers, "of
whom," writes Menendez, "I was in great need,"
were put on board the boat and sent to St. Augustine.
The rest were ordered to march thither by land.

The Adelantado walked in advance till he came to
a lonely spot, not far distant, deep among the bush-
covered hills.   Here he stopped, and with his cane
drew a line in the sand.   The sun was set when the
captive Huguenots, with their escort, reached the
fatal goal thus marked out.   And now let the curtain
drop; for here, in the name of Heaven, the hounds
of hell were turned loose, and the savage soldiery,
like wolves in a sheepfold, rioted in slaughter.   Of
all that wretched company, not one was left alive.

"I had their hands tied behind their backs," writes

por la Gente que os degollamos quando ganamos el **Fuerte**; è ansi es
menester, que con las manos atràs, amarradas, marcheis de aqui à quatro
Leguas, donde yo tengo mi Real."   Solís, 87.

the chief criminal, "and themselves put to the knife. It appeared to me that, by thus chastising them, God our Lord and your Majesty were served; whereby in future this evil sect will leave us more free to plant the Gospel in these parts." [1]

Again Menendez returned triumphant to St. Augustine, and behind him marched his band of butchers, steeped in blood to the elbows, but still unsated. Great as had been his success, he still had cause for anxiety. There was ill news of his fleet. Some of the ships were lost, others scattered, or lagging tardily on their way. Of his whole force, less than a half had reached Florida, and of these a large part were still at Fort Caroline. Ribaut could not be far off; and, whatever might be the condition of his shipwrecked company, their numbers would make them formidable, unless taken at advantage. Urged by fear and fortified by fanaticism, Menendez had well begun his work of slaughter; but rest for him there was none, — a darker deed was behind.

On the tenth of October, Indians came with the tidings that, at the spot where the first party of the shipwrecked French had been found, there was now another party still larger. This murder-loving race looked with great respect on Menendez for his wholesale butchery of the night before, — an exploit rarely equalled in their own annals of massacre. On his part, he doubted not that Ribaut was at hand. Marching with a hundred and fifty men, he crossed

---

[1] For the original, see *ante*, note 3, p. 137.

the bush-covered sands of Anastasia Island, followed the strand between the thickets and the sea, reached the inlet at midnight, and again, like a savage, ambushed himself on the bank. Day broke, and he could plainly see the French on the farther side. They had made a raft, which lay in the water ready for crossing.   Menendez and his men showed themselves, when, forthwith, the French displayed their banners, sounded drums and trumpets, and set their sick and starving ranks in array of battle.   But the Adelantado, regardless of this warlike show, ordered his men to seat themselves at breakfast, while he with three officers walked unconcernedly along the shore. His coolness had its effect. The French blew a trumpet of parley, and showed a white flag. The Spaniards replied.   A Frenchman came out upon the raft, and, shouting across the water, asked that a Spanish envoy should be sent over.

"You have a raft," was the reply; "come yourselves."

An Indian canoe lay under the bank on the Spanish side. A French sailor swam to it, paddled back unmolested, and presently returned, bringing with him La Caille, Ribaut's sergeant-major. He told Menendez that the French were three hundred and fifty in all, and were on their way to Fort Caroline; and, like the officers of the former party, he begged for boats to aid them in crossing the river.

"My brother," said Menendez, "go and tell your general, that, if he wishes to speak with me, he may come with four or six companions, and that I pledge my word he shall go back safe." [1]

La Caille returned; and Ribaut, with eight gentlemen, soon came over in the canoe. Menendez met them courteously, caused wine and preserved fruits to be placed before them, — he had come well provisioned on his errand of blood, — and next led Ribaut to the reeking Golgotha, where, in heaps upon the sand, lay the corpses of his slaughtered followers. Ribaut was prepared for the spectacle, — La Caille had already seen it, — but he would not believe that Fort Caroline was taken till a part of the plunder was shown him. Then, mastering his despair, he turned to the conqueror. "What has befallen us," he said, "may one day befall you." And, urging that the kings of France and Spain were brothers and close friends, he begged, in the name of that friendship, that the Spaniard would aid him in conveying his followers home. Menendez gave him the same equivocal answer that he had given the former party, and Ribaut returned to consult with his officers. After three hours of absence, he came back in the canoe, and told the Adelantado that some of his people were ready to surrender at discretion, but that many refused.

"They can do as they please," was the reply.

In behalf of those who surrendered, Ribaut offered a ransom of a hundred thousand ducats.

"It would much grieve me," said Menendez, "not to accept it; for I have great need of it."

[1] Solís, 88.

Ribaut was much encouraged.   Menendez could scarcely forego such a prize, and he thought, says the Spanish narrator, that the lives of his followers would now be safe.   He asked to be allowed the night for deliberation, and at sunset recrossed the river. In the morning he reappeared among the Spaniards, and reported that two hundred of his men had retreated from the spot, but that the remaining hundred and fifty would surrender.[1]   At the same time he gave into the hands of Menendez the royal standard and other flags, with his sword, dagger, helmet, buckler, and the official seal given him by Coligny.   Menendez directed an officer to enter the boat and bring over the French by tens.   He next led Ribaut among the bushes behind the neighboring sand-hill, and ordered his hands to be bound fast. Then the scales fell from the prisoner's eyes.   Face to face his fate rose up before him.   He saw his followers and himself entrapped, — the dupes of words artfully framed to lure them to their ruin.   The day wore on; and, as band after band of prisoners was brought over, they were led behind the sand-hill out of sight from the farther shore, and bound like their general.   At length the transit was finished.   With bloodshot eyes and weapons bared, the Spaniards closed around their victims.

"Are you Catholics or Lutherans? and is there any one among you who will go to confession?"

Ribaut answered, "I and all here are of the Reformed Faith."

---

[1] Solís, 89.   Menendez speaks only of seventy.

And he recited the Psalm, "*Domine, memento mei.*"[1]

"We are of earth," he continued, "and to earth we must return; twenty years more or less can matter little;"[2] and, turning to the Adelantado, he bade him do his will.

The stony-hearted bigot gave the signal; and those who will may paint to themselves the horrors of the scene.

A few, however, were spared. "I saved," writes Menendez, "the lives of two young gentlemen of about eighteen years of age, as well as of three others, the fifer, the drummer, and the trumpeter; and I caused Juan Ribao [Ribaut] with all the rest to be put to the knife, judging this to be necessary for the service of God our Lord and of your Majesty. And I consider it great good fortune that he [Juan Ribao] should be dead, for the King of France could effect more with him and five hundred ducats than with other men and five thousand; and he would do more in one year than another in ten, for he was the most experienced sailor and naval commander known, and of great skill in this navigation of the Indies and the coast of Florida. He was, besides, greatly liked in England, in which kingdom his reputation was such that he was appointed Captain-General of all the

---

[1] "L'auteur a voulu dire apparemment, *Memento Domine David.* D'ailleurs Ribaut la récita sans doute en Français, à la manière des Protestans." — *Hist. Gen. des Voyages*, XIV. 446.

[2] "Dijo; que de Tierra eran, y que en Tierra se avian de bolver; ò veinte Años mas, ò menos, todo era una Cuenta." Solís, 89.

English fleet against the French Catholics in the war between England and France some years ago." [1]

Such is the sum of the Spanish accounts, — the self-damning testimony of the author and abettors of the crime; a picture of lurid and awful coloring; and yet there is reason to believe that the truth was darker still. Among those who were spared was one Christophe le Breton, who was carried to Spain, escaped to France, and told his story to Challeux. Among those struck down in the butchery was a sailor of Dieppe, stunned and left for dead under a heap of corpses. In the night he revived, contrived to draw his knife, cut the cords that bound his hands, and made his way to an Indian village. The Indians, not without reluctance, abandoned him to the Spaniards, who sold him as a slave; but, on his way in fetters to Portugal, the ship was taken by the Huguenots, the sailor set free, and his story published in the narrative of Le Moyne. When the massacre was known in France, the friends and rela-

---

[1] "Salvé la vida à dos mozos Caballeros de hasta 18 años, y à otros tres, que eran Pifano, Atambor y Trompeta, y à Juan Rivao con todos los demas hice pasar à cuchillo, entendiendo que ansi convenia al servicio de Dios Nuestro Señor, y de V. Mag. y tengo por muy principal suerte que este sea muerto, porque mas hiciera el Rey de Francia con el con 500 ducados, que con otros con 5000, y mas hiciera el en un año que otro en diez, porque era el mas pratico marinero y cosario que se sabia, y muy diestro en esta Navigacion de Indias y costa de la Florida, y tan amigo en Inglaterra que tenia en aquel Reyno tanta reputacion que fué nombrado por Capitan General de toda el Armada Inglesa contra los Catolicos de Francia estos años pasados habiendo guerra entre Inglaterra y Francia." —*Carta de Pedro Menendez á su Magestad Fuerte de Sⁿ Agustin*, 15 de Octubre, 1565.

tives of the victims sent to the King, Charles the Ninth, a vehement petition for redress; and their memorial recounts many incidents of the tragedy. From these three sources is to be drawn the French version of the story.   The following is its substance.

Famished and desperate, the followers of Ribaut were toiling northward to seek refuge at Fort Caroline, when they found the Spaniards in their path. Some were filled with dismay; others, in their misery, almost hailed them as deliverers.   La Caille, the sergeant-major, crossed the river.   Menendez met him with a face of friendship, and protested that he would spare the lives of the shipwrecked men, sealing the promise with an oath, a kiss, and many signs of the cross.   He even gave it in writing, under seal.   Still, there were many among the French who would not place themselves in his power.   The most credulous crossed the river in a boat.   As each successive party landed, their hands were bound fast at their backs; and thus, except a few who were set apart, they were all driven towards the fort, like cattle to the shambles, with curses and scurrilous abuse.   Then, at sound of drums and trumpets, the Spaniards fell upon them, striking them down with swords, pikes, and halberds.[1]

[1] Here the French accounts differ. Le Moyne says that only a drummer and a fifer were spared; Challeux, that carpenters, artillerymen, and others who might be of use, were also saved, — thirty in all. Le Moyne speaks of the massacre as taking place, not at St. Augustine, but at Fort Caroline, a blunder into which, under the circumstances, he might naturally fall.

" . . . ainsi comme on feroit vn trouppeau de bestes lequel on

Ribaut vainly called on the Adelantado to remember his oath.   By his order, a soldier plunged a dagger into the French commander's heart; and Ottigny, who stood near, met a similar fate.   Ribaut's beard was cut off, and portions of it sent in a letter to Philip the Second.   His head was hewn into four parts, one of which was displayed on the point of a lance at each corner of Fort St. Augustine.   Great fires were kindled, and the bodies of the murdered burned to ashes.[1]

Such is the sum of the French accounts.   The charge of breach of faith contained in them was believed by Catholics as well as Protestants; and it was as a defence against this charge that the narrative of the Adelantado's brother-in-law was published.   That Ribaut, a man whose good sense and courage were both reputed high, should have sub-

chasseroit à la boucherie, lors à son de phiffres, tabourins et trompes, la hardiesse de ces furieux Espagnols se desbende sur ces poures François lesquels estoyent liez et garottez: là c'estoit à qui donneroit le plus beau cousp de picque, de hallebarde et d'espée," etc.   Challeux, from Christophe le Breton.

[1] " *Une Requête au Roy, faite en forme de Complainte par les Femmes veufves, petits Enfans orphelins, et autres leurs Amis, Parents et Alliez de ceux qui ont été cruellement envahis par les Espagnols en la France Antharctique dite la Floride.*"   This is the petition to Charles the Ninth.   There are Latin translations in De Bry and Chauveton. Christophe le Breton told Challeux the same story of the outrages on Ribaut's body.   The *Requête au Roy* affirms that the total number of French killed by the Spaniards in Florida in 1565 was more than nine hundred.   This is no doubt a gross exaggeration.

Prévost, a contemporary, Lescarbot, and others, affirm that Ribaut's body was flayed, and the skin sent to Spain as a trophy.   This is denied by Barcia.

mitted himself and his men to Menendez without positive assurance of safety, is scarcely credible; nor is it lack of charity to believe that a bigot so savage in heart and so perverted in conscience would act on the maxim, current among certain casuists of the day, that faith ought not to be kept with heretics.

It was night when the Adelantado again entered St. Augustine. There were some who blamed his cruelty; but many applauded. "Even if the French had been Catholics," — such was their language, — "he would have done right, for, with the little provision we have, they would all have starved; besides, there were so many of them that they would have cut our throats."

And now Menendez again addressed himself to the despatch, already begun, in which he recounts to the King his labors and his triumphs, a deliberate and business-like document, mingling narratives of butchery with recommendations for promotions, commissary details, and petitions for supplies, — enlarging, too, on the vast schemes of encroachment which his successful generalship had brought to naught. The French, he says, had planned a military and naval depot at Los Martires, whence they would make a descent upon Havana, and another at the Bay of Ponce de Leon, whence they could threaten Vera Cruz. They had long been encroaching on Spanish rights at Newfoundland, from which a great arm of the sea — doubtless meaning the St. Lawrence — would give them access to the Moluccas and other

parts of the East Indies. He adds, in a later
despatch, that by this passage they may reach the
mines of Zacatecas and St. Martin, as well as every
part of the South Sea. And, as already mentioned,
he urges immediate occupation of Chesapeake Bay,
which, by its supposed water communication with
the St. Lawrence, would enable Spain to vindicate
her rights, control the fisheries of Newfoundland,
and thwart her rival in vast designs of commercial and territorial aggrandizement. Thus did
France and Spain dispute the possession of North
America long before England became a party to the
strife.[1]

Some twenty days after Menendez returned to St.
Augustine, the Indians, enamoured of carnage, and
exulting to see their invaders mowed down, came to
tell him that on the coast southward, near Cape
Canaveral, a great number of Frenchmen were
intrenching themselves. They were those of Ribaut's
party who had refused to surrender. Having retreated
to the spot where their ships had been cast ashore,

---

[1] Amid all the confusion of his geographical statements, it seems
clear that Menendez believed that Chesapeake Bay communicated with
the St. Lawrence, and thence with Newfoundland on the one hand, and
the South Sea on the other. The notion that the St. Lawrence would
give access to China survived till the time of La Salle, or more than a
century. In the map of Gastaldi, made, according to Kohl, about
1550, a belt of water connecting the St. Lawrence and the Atlantic is
laid down. So also in the map of Ruscelli, 1561, and that of Martines,
1578, as well as in that of Michael Lok, 1582. In Munster's map, 1545,
the St. Lawrence is rudely indicated, with the words, "Per hoc fretū
iter ad Molucas."

they were trying to build a vessel from the fragments of the wrecks.

In all haste Menendez despatched messengers to Fort Caroline, — named by him San Mateo, — ordering a reinforcement of a hundred and fifty men. In a few days they came. He added some of his own soldiers, and, with a united force of two hundred and fifty, set out, as he tells us, on the second of November. A part of his force went by sea, while the rest pushed southward along the shore with such merciless energy that several men dropped dead with wading night and day through the loose sands. When, from behind their frail defences, the French saw the Spanish pikes and partisans glittering into view, they fled in a panic, and took refuge among the hills. Menendez sent a trumpet to summon them, pledging his honor for their safety. The commander and several others told the messenger that they would sooner be eaten by the savages than trust themselves to Spaniards; and, escaping, they fled to the Indian towns. The rest surrendered; and Menendez kept his word. The comparative number of his own men made his prisoners no longer dangerous. They were led back to St. Augustine, where, as the Spanish writer affirms, they were well treated. Those of good birth sat at the Adelantado's table, eating the bread of a homicide crimsoned with the slaughter of their comrades. The priests essayed their pious efforts, and, under the gloomy menace of the Inqui- sition, some of the heretics renounced their errors.

The fate of the captives may be gathered from the indorsement, in the handwriting of the King, on one of the despatches of Menendez.

"Say to him," writes Philip the Second, "that, as to those he has killed, he has done well; and as to those he has saved, they shall be sent to the galleys." [1]

[1] There is an indorsement to this effect on the despatch of Menendez of 12 December, 1565. A marginal note by the copyist states that it is in the well-known handwriting of Philip the Second. Compare the King's letter to Menendez, in Barcia, 116. This letter seems to have been written by a secretary in pursuance of a direction contained in the indorsement, — "Esto serà bien escribir luego à Pero Menendez," —and highly commends him for the "justice he has done upon the Lutheran corsairs."

CHAPTER IX.

1565–1567.

CHARLES IX. AND PHILIP II.

STATE OF INTERNATIONAL RELATIONS. — COMPLAINTS OF PHILIP
THE SECOND. — REPLY OF CHARLES THE NINTH. — NEWS OF
THE MASSACRE. — THE FRENCH COURT DEMANDS REDRESS. —
THE SPANISH COURT REFUSES IT.

THE state of international relations in the sixteenth
century is hardly conceivable at this day. The Puritans of England and the Huguenots of France
regarded Spain as their natural enemy, and on the
high seas and in the British Channel they joined
hands with godless freebooters to rifle her ships, kill
her sailors, or throw them alive into the sea. Spain
on her side seized English Protestant sailors who
ventured into her ports, and burned them as heretics,
or consigned them to a living death in the dungeons
of the Inquisition. Yet in the latter half of the
century these mutual outrages went on for years
while the nations professed to be at peace. There
was complaint, protest, and occasional menace, but
no redress, and no declaration of war.

Contemporary writers of good authority have said
that, when the news of the massacres in Florida
reached the court of France, Charles the Ninth and

Catherine de Medicis submitted to the insult in silence; but documents lately brought to light show that a demand for redress was made, though not insisted on. A cry of horror and execration had risen from the Huguenots, and many even of the Catholics had echoed it; yet the perpetrators of the crime, and not its victims, were the first to make complaint. Philip the Second resented the expeditions of Ribaut and Laudonnière as an invasion of the American domains of Spain, and ordered D'Alava, his ambassador at Paris, to denounce them to the French King. Charles, thus put on the defensive, replied, that the country in question belonged to France, having been discovered by Frenchmen a hundred years before, and named by them Terre des Bretons.[1] This alludes to the tradition that the Bretons and Basques visited the northern coasts of America before the voyage of Columbus. In several maps of the sixteenth century the region of New England and the neighboring states and provinces is set down as Terre des Bretons, or Tierra de los Bretones,[2] and this name was assumed by Charles to extend to the Gulf of Mexico, as the name of Florida was assumed by the Spaniards to extend to the Gulf of St. Lawrence, and even beyond it.[3] Philip spurned

[1] *Note de Charles IX. en réponse à celle de l'Ambassadeur d'Espagne,* in Gaffarel, *Floride,* 413.

[2] See, for example, the map of Ruscelli, 1561.

[3] "Il y a plus de cent ans a esté ledict païs appellé la terre des Bretons en laquelle est comprins l'endroit que les Espaignols s'attribuent, lequel ils ont baptizé du nom qu'ils ont voulu [*Florida*]." —

the claim, asserted the Spanish right to all Florida, and asked whether or not the followers of Ribaut and Laudonnière had gone thither by authority of their King. The Queen Mother, Catherine de Medicis, replied in her son's behalf, that certain Frenchmen had gone to a country called Terre aux Bretons, discovered by French subjects, and that in so doing they had been warned not to encroach on lands belonging to the King of Spain. And she added, with some spirit, that the Kings of France were not in the habit of permitting themselves to be threatened.[1]

Philip persisted in his attitude of injured innocence; and Forquevaulx, French ambassador at Madrid, reported that, as a reward for murdering French subjects, Menendez was to receive the title of Marquis of Florida. A demand soon followed from Philip, that Admiral Coligny should be punished for planting a French colony on Spanish ground, and thus causing the disasters that ensued. It was at this time that the first full account of the massacres reached the French court, and the Queen Mother, greatly moved, complained to the Spanish ambassador, saying that she could not persuade herself that his master would refuse reparation. The

Forquevaulx au Roy, 16 *Mars,* 1566. Forquevaulx was French ambassador at Madrid.

"Nous ne pretendons rien que conserver une terre qui a esté descouverte et possédée par des François, comme le nom de la terre aux Bretons le tesmoigne encore." — *Catherine de Médicis à Forquevaulx,* 30 *Dec.,* 1585.

[1] *Catherine de Médicis à Forquevaulx,* 20 *Jan.,* 1566.

ambassador replied by again throwing the blame on Coligny and the Huguenots; and Catherine de Medicis returned that, Huguenots or not, the King of Spain had no right to take upon himself the punishment of French subjects. Forquevaulx was instructed to demand redress at Madrid; but Philip only answered that he was very sorry for what had happened,[1] and again insisted that Coligny should be punished as the true cause of it.

Forquevaulx, an old soldier, remonstrated with firmness, declared that no deeds so execrable had ever been committed within his memory, and demanded that Menendez and his followers should be chastised as they deserved. The King said that he was sorry that the sufferers chanced to be Frenchmen, but, as they were pirates also, they ought to be treated as such. The ambassador replied, that they were no pirates, since they bore the commission of the Admiral of France, who in naval affairs represented the King; and Philip closed the conversation by saying that he would speak on the subject with the Duke of Alva. This was equivalent to refusal, for the views of the Duke were well known; "and so, Madame," writes the ambassador to the Queen Mother, "there is no hope that any reparation will be made for the aforesaid massacre."[2]

On this, Charles wrote to Forquevaulx: "It is my

---

[1] "Disant avoir santi grand desplaisir du faict advenu; voilà tout, Sire." — *Forquevaulx au Roy,* 9 *Avril,* 1566.

[2] *Forquevaulx à Catherine de Médicis,* 9 *Avril,* 1566.

will that you renew your complaint, and insist urgently that, for the sake of the union and friendship between the two crowns, reparation be made for the wrong done me and the cruelties committed on my subjects, to which I cannot submit without too great loss of reputation."[1] And, jointly with his mother, he ordered the ambassador to demand once more that Menendez and his men should be punished, adding, that he trusts that Philip will grant justice to the King of France, his brother-in-law and friend, rather than pardon a gang of brigands. "On this demand," concludes Charles, "the Sieur de Forquevaulx will not fail to insist, be the answer what it may, in order that the King of Spain shall understand that his Majesty of France has no less spirit than his predecessors to repel an insult."[2] The ambassador fulfilled his commission, and Philip replied by referring him to the Duke of Alva. "I have no hope," reports Forquevaulx, "that the Duke will give any satisfaction as to the massacre, for it was he who advised it from the first."[3] A year passed, and then he reported that Menendez had returned from Florida, that the King had given him a warm welcome, and that his fame as a naval commander was such that he was regarded as a sort of Neptune.[4]

In spite of their brave words, Charles and the

[1] *Charles IX. à Forquevaulx, 12 Mai, 1566.*

[2] *Mémoire envoyé par Charles IX. et Catherine de Médicis à Forquevaulx, 12 Mai, 1566.*

[3] *Forquevaulx au Roy, Août* (?), *1566.*

[4] *Forquevaulx au Roy, Juillet, 1567. Ibid., 2 Août, 1567.*

Queen Mother tamely resigned themselves to the affront, for they would not quarrel with Spain. To have done so would have been to throw themselves into the arms of the Protestant party, adopt the principle of toleration, and save France from the disgrace and blight of her later years. France was not so fortunate. The enterprise of Florida was a national enterprise, undertaken at the national charge, with the royal commission, and under the royal standard; and it had been crushed in time of peace by a power professing the closest friendship. Yet Huguenot influence had prompted and Huguenot hands executed it. That influence had now ebbed low; Coligny's power had waned; Charles, after long vacillation, was leaning more and more towards the Guises and the Catholics, and fast subsiding into the deathly embrace of Spain, for whom, at last, on the bloody eve of St. Bartholomew, he was to become the assassin of his own best subjects.[1]

In vain the relatives of the slain petitioned him for redress; and had the honor of the nation rested in the keeping of its King, the blood of hundreds of murdered Frenchmen would have cried from the ground in vain. But it was not to be so. Injured humanity found an avenger, and outraged France a champion. Her chivalrous annals may be searched in vain for a deed of more romantic daring than the vengeance of Dominique de Gourgues.

---

[1] *Lettres et Papiers d'Estat du Sieur de Forquevaulx, Ambassadeur du Roy très-Chrestien Charles Neufviesme,* printed by Gaffarel in his *Histoire de la Floride Française.*

CHAPTER X.

1567–1583.

DOMINIQUE DE GOURGUES.

THERE was a gentleman of Mont-de-Marsan,
Dominique de Gourgues, a soldier of ancient birth
and high renown. It is not certain that he was a
Huguenot. The Spanish annalist calls him a "terrible heretic;"[1] but the French Jesuit, Charlevoix,
anxious that the faithful should share the glory of
his exploits, affirms that, like his ancestors before
him, he was a good Catholic.[2] If so, his faith sat
lightly upon him; and, Catholic or heretic, he hated
the Spaniards with a mortal hate. Fighting in the
Italian wars, — for from boyhood he was wedded to

---

[1] Barcia, 133.

[2] Charlevoix, *Nouvelle France*, I. 95. Compare Guérin, *Navigateurs
Français*, 200. One of De Gourgues's descendants, the Vicomte A. de
Gourgues, has recently (1861) written an article to prove the Catholicity
of his ancestor.

the sword, — he had been taken prisoner by them
near Siena, where he had signalized himself by a fiery
and determined bravery.   With brutal insult, they
chained him to the oar as a galley slave.[1]   After he
had long endured this ignominy, the Turks captured
the vessel and carried her to Constantinople.   It was
but a change of tyrants; but, soon after, while she
was on a cruise, Gourgues still at the oar, a galley of
the knights of Malta hove in sight, bore down on her,
recaptured her, and set the prisoner free.   For several
years after, his restless spirit found employment in
voyages to Africa, Brazil, and regions yet more
remote.   His naval repute rose high, but his grudge
against the Spaniards still rankled within him; and
when, returned from his rovings, he learned the
tidings from Florida, his hot Gascon blood boiled
with fury.

The honor of France had been foully stained, and
there was none to wipe away the shame.   The fac-
tion-ridden King was dumb.   The nobles who surrounded him were in the Spanish interest.[2]   Then,
since they proved recreant, he, Dominique de
Gourgues, a simple gentleman, would take upon him
to avenge the wrong, and restore the dimmed lustre
of the French name.[3]   He sold his inheritance, bor-

---

[1] Lescarbot, *Nouvelle France*, I. 141 ; Barcia, 133.

[2] It was at this time that the Duc de Montpensier was heard to say,
that, if his heart was opened, the name of Philip would be found
written in it.   Ranke, *Civil Wars*, I. 337.

[3] " El, encendido en el Celo de la Honra de su Patria, avia deter-
minado gastar su Hacienda en aquella Empresa, de que no esperaba

rowed money from his brother, who held a high post in Guienne,[1] and equipped three small vessels, navigable by sail or oar. On board he placed a hundred arquebusiers and eighty sailors, prepared to fight on land, if need were.[2] The noted Blaise de Montluc, then lieutenant for the King in Guienne, gave him a commission to make war on the negroes of Benin, — that is, to kidnap them as slaves, an adventure then held honorable.[3]

His true design was locked within his own breast. He mustered his followers, — not a few of whom were of rank equal to his own, — feasted them, and, on the twenty-second of August, 1567, sailed from the mouth of the Charente. Off Cape Finisterre, so violent a storm buffeted his ships that his men clam-

mas fruto, que vengarse, para eternizar su Fama." Barcia, 134. This is the statement of an enemy. A contemporary manuscript preserved in the Gourgues family makes a similar statement.

[1] " . . . era Presidente de la Generalidad de Guiena." Barcia, 133. Compare Mezeray, *Hist. of France*, 701. There is repeated mention of him in the Memoirs of Montluc.

[2] De Gourgues MS. Barcia says two hundred; Basanier and Lescarbot, a hundred and fifty.

[3] De Gourgues MS. This is a copy, made in 1831, by the Vicomte de Gourgues, from the original preserved in the Gourgues family, and written either by Dominique de Gourgues himself, or by some person to whom he was intimately known. It is, with but trifling variations, identical with the two narratives entitled *La Reprinse de la Floride*, preserved in the Bibliothèque Impériale. One of these bears the name of Robert Prévost, but whether as author or copyist is not clear. M. Gaillard, who carefully compared them, has written a notice of their contents, with remarks. The Prévost narrative has been printed entire by Ternaux-Compans in his collection. I am indebted to Mr. Bancroft for the use of the Vicomte de Gourgues's copy, and Gaillard's notice.

ored to return; but Gourgues's spirit prevailed. He
bore away for Africa, and, landing at the Rio del
Oro, refreshed and cheered them as he best might.
Thence he sailed to Cape Blanco, where the jealous
Portuguese, who had a fort in the neighborhood, set
upon him three negro chiefs. Gourgues beat them
off, and remained master of the harbor; whence, however, he soon voyaged onward to Cape Verd, and,
steering westward, made for the West Indies. Here,
advancing from island to island, he came to Hispaniola, where, between the fury of a hurricane at sea
and the jealousy of the Spaniards on shore, he was in
no small jeopardy, — "the Spaniards," exclaims the
indignant journalist, "who think that this New
World was made for nobody but them, and that no
other living man has a right to move or breathe
here!" Gourgues landed, however, obtained the
water of which he was in need, and steered for Cape
San Antonio, at the western end of Cuba. There he
gathered his followers about him, and addressed them
with his fiery Gascon eloquence. For the first time,
he told them his true purpose, inveighed against
Spanish cruelty, and painted, with angry rhetoric,
the butcheries of Fort Caroline and St. Augustine.

"What disgrace," he cried, "if such an insult
should pass unpunished! What glory to us if we
avenge it! To this I have devoted my fortune. I
relied on you. I thought you jealous enough of your
country's glory to sacrifice life itself in a cause like
this. Was I deceived? I will show you the way;

I will be always at your head; I will bear the brunt of the danger. Will you refuse to follow me?"[1]

At first his startled hearers listened in silence; but soon the passions of that adventurous age rose responsive to his words. The combustible French nature burst into flame. The enthusiasm of the soldiers rose to such a pitch that Gourgues had much ado to make them wait till the moon was full before tempting the perils of the Bahama Channel. His time came at length. The moon rode high above the lonely sea, and, silvered in its light, the ships of the avenger held their course.

Meanwhile, it had fared ill with the Spaniards in Florida; the good-will of the Indians had vanished. The French had been obtrusive and vexatious guests; but their worst trespasses had been mercy and tenderness compared to the daily outrage of the new-comers. Friendship had changed to aversion, aversion to hatred, and hatred to open war. The forest paths were beset; stragglers were cut off; and woe to the Spaniard who should venture after nightfall beyond call of the outposts.[2]

Menendez, however, had strengthened himself in his new conquest. St. Augustine was well fortified; Fort Caroline, now Fort San Mateo, was repaired;

---

[1] The De Gourgues MS., with Prévost and Gaillard, give the speech in substance. Charlevoix professes to give a part in the words of the speaker: "J'ai compté sur vous, je vous ai cru assez jaloux de la gloire de votre Patrie, pour lui sacrifier jusqu'à votre vie en une occasion de cette importance; me suis-je trompé?" etc.

[2] Barcia, 100–130.

and two redoubts, or small forts, were thrown up to guard the mouth of the River of May, — one of them near the present lighthouse at Mayport, and the other across the river on Fort George Island. Thence, on an afternoon in early spring, the Spaniards saw three sail steering northward. They suspected no enemy, and their batteries boomed a salute. Gourgues's ships replied, then stood out to sea, and were lost in the shades of evening.

They kept their course all night, and, as day broke, anchored at the mouth of a river, the St. Mary's, or the Santilla, by their reckoning fifteen leagues north of the River of May. Here, as it grew light, Gourgues saw the borders of the sea thronged with savages, armed and plumed for war. They, too, had mistaken the strangers for Spaniards, and mustered to meet their tyrants at the landing. But in the French ships there was a trumpeter who had been long in Florida, and knew the Indians well. He went towards them in a boat, with many gestures of friendship; and no sooner was he recognized, than the naked crowd, with yelps of delight, danced for joy along the sands. Why had he ever left them? they asked; and why had he not returned before? The intercourse thus auspiciously begun was actively kept up. Gourgues told the principal chief, — who was no other than Satouriona, once the ally of the French, — that he had come to visit them, make friendship with them, and bring them presents. At this last announcement, so grateful to Indian ears, the dancing was renewed with double zeal. The next morning was named for a grand council, and Satouriona sent runners to summon all Indians within call; while Gourgues, for safety, brought his vessels within the mouth of the river.

Morning came, and the woods were thronged with warriors. Gourgues and his soldiers landed with martial pomp. In token of mutual confidence, the French laid aside their arquebuses, and the Indians their bows and arrows. Satouriona came to meet the strangers, and seated their commander at his side, on a wooden stool, draped and cushioned with the gray Spanish moss. Two old Indians cleared the spot of brambles, weeds, and grass; and, when their task was finished, the tribesmen took their places, ring within ring, standing, sitting, and crouching on the ground, — a dusky concourse, plumed in festal array, waiting with grave visages and intent eyes. Gourgues was about to speak, when the chief, who, says the narrator, had not learned French manners, anticipated him, and broke into a vehement harangue, denouncing the cruelty of the Spaniards.

Since the French fort was taken, he said, the Indians had not had one happy day. The Spaniards drove them from their cabins, stole their corn, ravished their wives and daughters, and killed their children; and all this they had endured because they loved the French. There was a French boy who had escaped from the massacre at the fort; they had found him in the woods; and though the Spaniards, who wished to kill him, demanded that they should give him up, they had kept him for his friends.

"Look!" pursued the chief, "here he is!" — and he brought forward a youth of sixteen, named Pierre Debré, who became at once of the greatest service to the French, his knowledge of the Indian language making him an excellent interpreter.[1]

Delighted as he was at this outburst against the Spaniards, Gourgues did not see fit to display the full extent of his satisfaction. He thanked the Indians for their good-will, exhorted them to continue in it, and pronounced an ill-merited eulogy on the greatness and goodness of his King. As for the Spaniards, he said, their day of reckoning was at hand; and, if the Indians had been abused for their love of the French, the French would be their avengers. Here Satouriona forgot his dignity, and leaped up for joy.

"What!" he cried, "will you fight the Spaniards?"[2]

"I came here," replied Gourgues, "only to reconnoitre the country and make friends with you, and then go back to bring more soldiers; but, when I hear what you are suffering from them, I wish to fall upon them this very day, and rescue you from their tyranny." All around the ring a clamor of applauding voices greeted his words.

[1] De Gourgues MS.; Gaillard MS.; Basanier, 116; Barcia, 134.

[2] ". . . si les rois et leurs sujects avoient esté maltraictez en haine des François que aussi seroient-ils vengez par les François-mesmes. Comment? dist Satirona, tressaillant d'aise, vouldriez-vous bien faire la guerre aux Espaignols?" — *De Gourgues MS.*

"But you will do your part," pursued the Frenchman; "you will not leave us all the honor."

"We will go," replied Satouriona, "and die with
you, if need be."

"Then, if we fight, we ought to fight at once.
How soon can you have your warriors ready to
march?"

The chief asked three days for preparation.
Gourgues cautioned him to secrecy, lest the Spaniards should take alarm.

"Never fear," was the answer; "we hate them
more than you do." [1]

Then came a distribution of gifts, — knives,
hatchets, mirrors, bells, and beads, — while the warrior rabble crowded to receive them, with eager
faces and outstretched arms. The distribution over,
Gourgues asked the chiefs if there was any other
matter in which he could serve them. On this, point-
ing to his shirt, they expressed a peculiar admiration
for that garment, and begged each to have one, to be
worn at feasts and councils during life, and in their

---

[1] The above is a condensation from the original narrative, of the
style of which the following may serve as an example : " Le cappitaine
Gourgue qui avoit trouvé ce qu'il chercheoit, les louë et remercie
grandement, et pour battre le fer pendant qu'il estoit chault leur dist :
Voiremais si nous voullons leur faire la guerre, il fauldroit que ce fust
incontinant. Dans combien de temps pourriez-vous bien avoir assemblé
voz gens prets à marcher ? Dans trois jours dist Satirona, nous et nos
subjects pourrons nous rendre icy, pour partir avec vous. Et ce pendant (dist le cappitaine Gourgue), vous donnerez bon ordre que le tout
soit tenu secrect : affin que les Espaignols n'en puissent sentir le vent.
Ne vous soulciez, dirent les rois, nous leur voullons plus de mal que
vous," etc., etc.

graves after death. Gourgues complied; and his grateful confederates were soon stalking about him, fluttering in the spoils of his wardrobe.

To learn the strength and position of the Spaniards, Gourgues now sent out three scouts; and with them went Olotoraca, Satouriona's nephew, a young brave of great renown.

The chief, eager to prove his good faith, gave as hostages his only surviving son and his favorite wife. They were sent on board the ships, while the Indians dispersed to their encampments, with leaping, stamping, dancing, and whoops of jubilation.

The day appointed came, and with it the savage army, hideous in war-paint, and plumed for battle. The woods rang back their songs and yells, as with frantic gesticulation they brandished their war-clubs and vaunted their deeds of prowess. Then they drank the black drink, endowed with mystic virtues against hardship and danger; and Gourgues himself pretended to swallow the nauseous decoction.[1]

These ceremonies consumed the day. It was even-

---

[1] The "black drink" was, till a recent period, in use among the Creeks. It is a strong decoction of the plant popularly called cassina, or uupon tea. Major Swan, deputy agent for the Creeks in 1791, thus describes their belief in its properties : "that it purifies them from all sin, and leaves them in a state of perfect innocence; that it inspires them with an invincible prowess in war ; and that it is the only solid cement of friendship, benevolence, and hospitality." Swan's account of their mode of drinking and ejecting it corresponds perfectly with Le Moyne's picture in De Bry. See the United States government publication, *History, Condition, and Prospects of Indian Tribes*, V. 266.

ing before the allies filed off into their forests, and
took the path for the Spanish forts. The French, on
their part, were to repair by sea to the rendezvous.
Gourgues mustered and addressed his men. It was
needless: their ardor was at fever height. They
broke in upon his words, and demanded to be led at
once against the enemy. François Bourdelais, with
twenty sailors, was left with the ships, and Gourgues
affectionately bade him farewell.

"If I am slain in this most just enterprise," he
said, "I leave all in your charge, and pray you to
carry back my soldiers to France."

There were many embracings among the excited
Frenchmen, — many sympathetic tears from those
who were to stay behind, — many messages left with
them for wives, children, friends, and mistresses;
and then this valiant band pushed their boats from
shore.[1] It was a hare-brained venture, for, as young
Debré had assured them, the Spaniards on the River
of May were four hundred in number, secure behind
their ramparts.[2]

Hour after hour the sailors pulled at the oar.
They glided slowly by the sombre shores in the shim-
mering moonlight, to the sound of the murmuring

---

[1] "Cecy attendrist fort le cueur de tous, et mesmement des mariniers
qui demeuroient pour la garde des navires, lesquels ne peurent contenir
leurs larmes, et fut ceste départie plaine de compassion d'ouïr tant
d'adieux d'une part et d'aultre, et tant de charges et recommendations
de la part de ceulx qui s'en alloient à leurs parents et amis, et à leurs
femmes et alliez au cas qu'ils ne retournassent." Prévost, 337.

[2] De Gourgues MS.; Basanier, 117; Charlevoix, I. 99.

surf and the moaning pine-trees. In the gray of the
morning, they came to the mouth of a river, probably
the Nassau; and here a northeast wind set in with
a violence that almost wrecked their boats. Their
Indian allies were waiting on the bank, but for a
while the gale delayed their crossing. The bolder
French would lose no time, rowed through the tossing waves, and, landing safely, left their boats, and
pushed into the forest. Gourgues took the lead, in
breastplate and back-piece. At his side marched the
young chief Olotoraca, with a French pike in his
hand; and the files of arquebuse-men and armed
sailors followed close behind. They plunged through
swamps, hewed their way through brambly thickets
and the matted intricacies of the forests, and, at five
in the afternoon, almost spent with fatigue and
hunger, came to a river or inlet of the sea,[1] not far
from the first Spanish fort. Here they found three
hundred Indians waiting for them.

Tired as he was, Gourgues would not rest. He
wished to attack at daybreak, and with ten arquebusiers and his Indian guide he set out to reconnoitre. Night closed upon him. It was a vain task
to struggle on, in pitchy darkness, among trunks of
trees, fallen logs, tangled vines, and swollen streams.
Gourgues returned, anxious and gloomy. An Indian
chief approached him, read through the darkness his
perturbed look, and offered to lead him by a better

[1] Talbot Inlet? Compare Sparks, *American Biography*, 2d Ser,
VII. 128.

path along the margin of the sea. Gourgues joyfully
assented, and ordered all his men to march. The
Indians, better skilled in wood-craft, chose the
shorter course through the forest.

The French forgot their weariness, and pressed on
with speed. At dawn they and their allies met on
the bank of a stream, probably Sister Creek, beyond
which, and very near, was the fort. But the tide
was in, and they tried in vain to cross. Greatly
vexed, — for he had hoped to take the enemy
asleep, — Gourgues withdrew his soldiers into the
forest, where they were no sooner ensconced than a
drenching rain fell, and they had much ado to keep
their gun-matches burning. The light grew fast.
Gourgues plainly saw the fort, the defences of which
seemed slight and unfinished. He even saw the
Spaniards at work within. A feverish interval
elapsed, till at length the tide was out, — so far, at
least, that the stream was fordable. A little higher
up, a clump of trees lay between it and the fort.
Behind this friendly screen the passage was begun.
Each man tied his powder-flask to his steel cap, held
his arquebuse above his head with one hand, and
grasped his sword with the other. The channel was
a bed of oysters. The sharp shells cut their feet as
they waded through. But the farther bank was
gained. They emerged from the water, drenched,
lacerated, and bleeding, but with unabated mettle.
Gourgues set them in array under cover of the trees.
They stood with kindling eyes, and hearts throbbing,

but not with fear.   Gourgues pointed to the Spanish
fort, seen by glimpses through the boughs.   "Look!"
he said, "there are the robbers who have stolen this
land from our King; there are the murderers who
have butchered our countrymen!"[1] With voices
eager, fierce, but half suppressed, they demanded to
be led on.

Gourgues gave the word.   Cazenove, his lieutenant, with thirty men, pushed for the fort gate; he
himself, with the main body, for the glacis.   It was
near noon; the Spaniards had just finished their
meal, and, says the narrative, "were still picking their
teeth," when a startled cry rang in their ears: —

"To arms! to arms!   The French are coming! the
French are coming!"

It was the voice of a cannoneer who had that
moment mounted the rampart and seen the assailants
advancing in unbroken ranks, with heads lowered and
weapons at the charge.   He fired his cannon among
them.   He even had time to load and fire again,
when the light-limbed Olotoraca bounded forward,
ran up the glacis, leaped the unfinished ditch, and
drove his pike through the Spaniard from breast to
back.   Gourgues was now on the glacis, when he
heard Cazenove shouting from the gate that the
Spaniards were escaping on that side.   He turned
and led his men thither at a run.   In a moment, the

---

[1] " . . . et, leur monstrant le fort qu'ils pouvoient entreveoir à
travers les arbres, voilà (dist il) les volleurs qui ont vollé ceste terre à
nostre Roy, voilà les meurtriers qui ont massacré nos françois." — *De
Gourgues MS.* Compare Charlevoix, I. 100.

fugitives, sixty in all, were enclosed between his party and that of his lieutenant. The Indians, too, came leaping to the spot. Not a Spaniard escaped. All were cut down but a few, reserved by Gourgues for a more inglorious end.[1]

Meanwhile the Spaniards in the other fort, on the opposite shore, cannonaded the victors without ceasing. The latter turned four captured guns against them. One of Gourgues's boats, a very large one, had been brought along-shore, and, entering it with eighty soldiers, he pushed for the farther bank. With loud yells, the Indians leaped into the river, which is here about three fourths of a mile wide. Each held his bow and arrows aloft in one hand, while he swam with the other. A panic seized the garrison as they saw the savage multitude. They broke out of the fort and fled into the forest. But the French had already landed; and, throwing themselves in the path of the fugitives, they greeted them with a storm of lead. The terrified wretches recoiled; but flight was vain. The Indian whoop rang behind them, and war-clubs and arrows finished the work. Gourgues's utmost efforts saved but fifteen, not out of mercy, but from a refinement of vengeance.[2]

The next day was Quasimodo Sunday, or the Sun-

---

[1] Barcia's Spanish account agrees with the De Gourgues MS., except in a statement of the former that the Indians had formed an ambuscade into which the Spaniards fell.

[2] It must be admitted that there is a strong savor of romance in the French narrative. The admissions of the Spanish annalist prove, however, that it has a broad basis of truth.

day after Easter. Gourgues and his men remained quiet, making ladders for the assault on Fort San Mateo. Meanwhile the whole forest was in arms, and, far and near, the Indians were wild with excitement. They beset the Spanish fort till not a soldier could venture out. The garrison, aware of their danger, though ignorant of its extent, devised an expedient to gain information; and one of them, painted and feathered like an Indian, ventured within Gourgues's outposts. He himself chanced to be at hand, and by his side walked his constant attendant, Olotoraca. The keen-eyed young savage pierced the cheat at a glance. The spy was seized, and, being examined, declared that there were two hundred and sixty Spaniards in San Mateo, and that they believed the French to be two thousand, and were so frightened that they did not know what they were doing.

Gourgues, well pleased, pushed on to attack them. On Monday evening he sent forward the Indians to ambush themselves on both sides of the fort. In the morning he followed with his Frenchmen; and, as the glittering ranks came into view, defiling between the forest and the river, the Spaniards opened on them with culverins from a projecting bastion. The French took cover in the woods with which the hills below and behind the fort were densely overgrown. Here, himself unseen, Gourgues could survey the whole extent of the defences, and he presently descried a strong party of Spaniards issuing from their works, crossing the ditch, and advancing to reconnoitre.

On this, he sent Cazenove, with a detachment, to station himself at a point well hidden by trees on the flank of the Spaniards, who, with strange infatuation, continued their advance. Gourgues and his followers pushed on through the thickets to meet them. As the Spaniards reached the edge of the open ground, a deadly fire blazed in their faces, and, before the smoke cleared, the French were among them, sword in hand. The survivors would have fled; but Cazenove's detachment fell upon their rear, and all were killed or taken.

When their comrades in the fort beheld their fate, a panic seized them. Conscious of their own deeds, perpetrated on this very spot, they could hope no mercy, and their terror multiplied immeasurably the numbers of their enemy. They abandoned the fort in a body, and fled into the woods most remote from the French. But here a deadlier foe awaited them; for a host of Indians leaped up from ambush. Then rose those hideous war-cries which have curdled the boldest blood and blanched the manliest cheek. The forest warriors, with savage ecstasy, wreaked their long arrears of vengeance, while the French hastened to the spot, and lent their swords to the slaughter. A few prisoners were saved alive; the rest were slain; and thus did the Spaniards make bloody atonement for the butchery of Fort Caroline.[1]

[1] This is the French account. The Spaniard Barcia, with greater probability, says that some of the Spaniards escaped to the hills. With this exception, the French and Spanish accounts agree. Barcia ascribes the defeat of his countrymen to an exaggerated idea of the

But Gourgues's vengeance was not yet appeased. Hard by the fort, the trees were pointed out to him on which Menendez had hanged his captives, and placed over them the inscription, "Not as to Frenchmen, but as to Lutherans."

Gourgues ordered the Spanish prisoners to be led thither.

"Did you think," he sternly said, as the pallid wretches stood ranged before him, "that so vile a treachery, so detestable a cruelty, against a King so potent and a nation so generous, would go unpunished? I, one of the humblest gentlemen among my King's subjects, have charged myself with avenging it.   Even if the Most Christian and the Most Catholic Kings had been enemies, at deadly war, such perfidy and extreme cruelty would still have been unpardonable.   Now that they are friends and close allies, there is no name vile enough to brand your deeds, no punishment sharp enough to requite them.   But though you cannot suffer as you deserve, you shall suffer all that an enemy can honorably inflict, that your example may teach others to observe the peace and alliance which you have so perfidiously violated." [1]

enemy's force.   The governor, Gonzalo de Villaroel, was, he says, among those who escaped.   I have purposely preserved in the narrative the somewhat exalted tone of the original French account.

[1] " . . . Mais encores que vous ne puissiez endurer la peine que vous avez méritée, il est besoin que vous enduriez celle que l'ennemy vous peult donner honnestement : affin que par vostre exemple les autres appreignent à garder la paix et alliance que si meschamment et malheureusement vous avez violée.   Cela dit, ils sont branchez aux mesmes arbres où ils avoient penduz les François." — *De Gourgues MS.*

They were hanged where the French had hung before them; and over them was nailed the inscription, burned with a hot iron on a tablet of pine, "Not as to Spaniards, but as to Traitors, Robbers, and Murderers."[1]

Gourgues's mission was fulfilled. To occupy the country had never been his intention; nor was it possible, for the Spaniards were still in force at St. Augustine. His was a whirlwind visitation, — to ravage, ruin, and vanish. He harangued the Indians, and exhorted them to demolish the fort. They fell to the work with eagerness, and in less than a day not one stone was left on another.[2]

Gourgues returned to the forts at the mouth of the river, destroyed them also, and took up his march for his ships. It was a triumphal procession. The Indians thronged around the victors with gifts of fish and game; and an old woman declared that she was now ready to die, since she had seen the French once more.

The ships were ready for sea. Gourgues bade his

[1] "Je ne faicts cecy comme à Espaignolz, n'y comme à Marannes ; mais comme à traistres, volleurs, et meurtriers." — *De Gourgues MS*.

Maranne, or *Marane*, was a word of reproach applied to Spaniards. It seems originally to have meant a Moor. Michelet calls Ferdinand of Spain " ce vieux Marane avare." The Spanish Pope, Alexander the Sixth, was always nicknamed *Le Marane* by his enemy and successor, Rovere.

On returning to the forts at the mouth of the river, Gourgues hanged all the prisoners he had left there. One of them, says the narrative, confessed that he had aided in hanging the French.

[2] "Ilz feirent telle diligence qu'en moings d'ung jour ilz ne laissèrent pierre sur pierre." — *De Gourgues MS*.

disconsolate allies farewell, and nothing would content them but a promise to return soon. Before embarking, he addressed his own men: —

"My friends, let us give thanks to God for the success He has granted us. It is He who saved us from tempests; it is He who inclined the hearts of the Indians towards us; it is He who blinded the understanding of the Spaniards. They were four to one, in forts well armed and provisioned. Our right was our only strength; and yet we have conquered. Not to our own swords, but to God only, we owe our victory. Then let us thank Him, my friends; let us never forget His favors; and let us pray that He may continue them, saving us from dangers, and guiding us safely home. Let us pray, too, that He may so dispose the hearts of men that our perils and toils may find favor in the eyes of our King and of all France, since all we have done was done for the King's service and for the honor of our country." [1]

Thus Spaniards and Frenchmen alike laid their reeking swords on God's altar.

Gourgues sailed on the third of May, and, gazing back along their foaming wake, the adventurers looked their last on the scene of their exploits. Their success had cost its price. A few of their number had fallen, and hardships still awaited the survivors. Gourgues, however, reached Rochelle on the day of Pentecost, and the Huguenot citizens

[1] De Gourgues MS.   The speech is a little condensed in the translation.

greeted him with all honor.   At court it fared worse
with him.   The King, still obsequious to Spain,
looked on him coldly and askance.   The Spanish
minister demanded his head.   It was hinted to him
that he was not safe, and he withdrew to Rouen,
where he found asylum among his friends.   His fortune was gone; debts contracted for his expedition
weighed heavily on him; and for years he lived in
obscurity, almost in misery.

At length his prospects brightened.   Elizabeth of
England learned his merits and his misfortunes, and
invited him to enter her service.   The King, who,
says the Jesuit historian, had always at heart been
delighted with his achievement,[1] openly restored him
to favor, while, some years later, Don Antonio
tendered him command of his fleet, to defend his
right to the crown of Portugal against Philip the
Second.   Gourgues, happy once more to cross swords
with the Spaniards, gladly embraced this offer; but
in 1583, on his way to join the Portuguese prince,
he died at Tours of a sudden illness.[2]   The French
mourned the loss of the man who had wiped a blot
from the national scutcheon, and respected his
memory as that of one of the best captains of his
time.   And, in truth, if a zealous patriotism, a fiery
valor, and skilful leadership are worthy of honor,
then is such a tribute due to Dominique de Gourgues,

---

[1] Charlevoix, *Nouvelle France*, I. 105.
[2] Basanier, 123 ; Lescarbot, 141 ; Barcia, 137 ; Gaillard, *Notice des Manuscrits de la Bibliothèque du Roi.*

slave-catcher and half-pirate as he was, like other naval heroes of that wild age.

Romantic as was his exploit, it lacked the fulness of poetic justice, since the chief offender escaped him. While Gourgues was sailing towards Florida, Menendez was in Spain, high in favor at court, where he told to approving ears how he had butchered the heretics. Borgia, the sainted General of the Jesuits, was his fast friend; and two years later, when he returned to America, the Pope, Paul the Fifth, regarding him as an instrument for the conversion of the Indians, wrote him a letter with his benediction.[1] He re-established his power in Florida, rebuilt Fort San Mateo, and taught the Indians that death or flight was the only refuge from Spanish tyranny. They murdered his missionaries and spurned their doctrine. "The Devil is the best thing in the world," they cried; "we adore him; he makes men brave." Even the Jesuits despaired, and abandoned Florida in disgust.

Menendez was summoned home, where fresh honors awaited him from the Crown, though, according to the somewhat doubtful assertion of the heretical Grotius, his deeds had left a stain upon his name among the people.[2] He was given command of the armada of three hundred sail and twenty thousand men, which, in 1574, was gathered at Santander against England and Flanders. But now, at the

---

[1] "Carta de San Pio V. à Pedro Menendez," Barcia, 139.
[2] Grotius, *Annales*, 63.

height of his fortunes, his career was abruptly closed. He died suddenly, at the age of fifty-five. Grotius affirms that he killed himself; but, in his eagerness to point the moral of his story, he seems to have overstepped the bounds of historic truth. The Spanish bigot was rarely a suicide; for the rites of Christian burial and repose in consecrated ground were denied to the remains of the self-murderer. There is positive evidence, too, in a codicil to the will of Menendez, dated at Santander on the fifteenth of September, 1574, that he was on that day seriously ill, though, as the instrument declares, "of sound mind." There is reason, then, to believe that this pious cut-throat died a natural death, crowned with honors, and soothed by the consolations of his religion.[1]

It was he who crushed French Protestantism in America. To plant religious freedom on this western soil was not the mission of France. It was for her to rear in northern forests the banner of absolutism and of Rome; while among the rocks of Massachusetts England and Calvin fronted her in dogged opposition.

Long before the ice-crusted pines of Plymouth had

[1] For a copy of portions of the will, and other interesting papers concerning Menendez, I am indebted to Buckingham Smith, Esq., whose patient and zealous research in the archives of Spain has thrown new light on Spanish North American history.

There is a brief notice of Menendez in De la Mota's *History of the Order of Santiago* (1599), and also another of later date written to accompany his engraved portrait. Neither of them conveys any hint of suicide.

Menendez was a Commander of the Order of Santiago.

listened to the rugged psalmody of the Puritan, the solitudes of Western New York and the stern wilderness of Lake Huron were trodden by the iron heel of the soldier and the sandalled foot of the Franciscan friar. France was the true pioneer of the Great West. They who bore the fleur-de-lis were always in the van, patient, daring, indomitable. And foremost on this bright roll of forest chivalry stands the half-forgotten name of Samuel de Champlain.

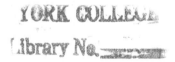